HOWARD RICKETTS

FIREARMS

OCTOPUS BOOKS

Acknowledgments

The author wishes to express his grateful thanks to the following people who have given him advice and help: his brother Michael, Captain Charles Adams, Claude Blair Esq, Philip Coole Esq, Miss Belinda Durbridge, Miss Fleming-Smith, Thomas Goff Esq, John Hayward Esq, Norris Kennard Esq, Captain John Laing, Mrs Vincent Lowson, the late Sir James Mann, Dr Sigurd Mauritz, Signor Luigi Mazzoli, Sir Harold Nicolson, Miss Elvira Niggerman, Freiherr Alexander von Reitzenstein, and John Sparrow Esq.

The author and publishers wish to thank the following owners and collectors who have made available objects from their collections: The Earl of Plymouth, figures 19, 53, 101, 109, 110, 112, 115; Lord Braybrooke, figure 105; Clay P. Bedford Esq, figures 77, 86; Thomas Goff Esq, figure 130; Loel Guinness Esq, figure 52; Harmer Johnson Esq, figure 125; Anthony Opie Esq, figure 16; W. J. Ward Esq, the endpapers and figure 102.

The following photographs are reproduced by permission of Messrs Sotheby & Co: figures 1, 8, 9, 10, 12, 15, 16, 19, 21, 22, 24, 28, 30, 34, 37a, 38, 41, 46, 48, 53, 55, 58, 59, 61, 62, 63, 66, 67, 72, 74, 75, 76, 77, 79, 80, 81, 84, 88, 89, 92, 95, 96, 98, 100, 101, 103, 104, 109, 110, 114, 115, 116, 117, 118, 120, 123, 125, 126, 128, 129, 131, 132, 133, 135, 137, 138, 139, 140.

The following photographs are reproduced by courtesy of the following museums and art galleries: the British Museum, figures 2, 4, 7, 18, 44, 97, 127; the Governing Body of Christ Church, Oxford, figure 5; the National Bavarian Museum, Munich, figures 11, 33, 50, 60, 64, 65, 90, 91, 93, 94, 106, 111; the National Gallery, London, figure 51; the National Portrait Gallery, London, figure 56; the Royal United Services Institute Museum, Whitehall, figures 17, 69, 70, 71, 85, 87, 107, 108, 121, 122, 134; the Tate Gallery, London, figure 52; the Tower of London, figures 3, 13, 25, 31, 47, 82, 83, 105, 124; the Victoria and Albert Museum, London, figures 14, 20, 27, 35, 36, 37, 40, 42, 43, 45, 49, 54, 57, 68, 99, 119; the Wallace Collection, London, figures 32, 39, 78.

Figure 23 was photographed by Claude Blair; figures 3, 12, 17, 26, 30, 31, 37, 45, 47, 57, 66, 69, 71, 83, 85, 87, 99, 100, 101, 103, 105, 107, 108, 112, 116, 120, 121, 122, 130, 134, 135 by Messrs A. C. Cooper; figure 73 by Tom Scott; figures 1, 9, 19, 70, 75, 84, 88, 128, 129, 131, 132, 133, 139, 140 by Messrs Sperryns Ltd; figures 11, 33, 60, 64, 65, 90, 93, 94, 106, 111 by Herbert Weissmann; figure 53 by Ken Wood, figure 14 by Diana Wyllie Ltd.

This edition first published 1972 by
OCTOPUS BOOKS LIMITED

59 Grosvenor Street, London W.1

ISBN 7064 0041 0

Preceding page
Two Italian flintlock pistols set into the covers of a Bible

PRODUCED BY MANDARIN PUBLISHERS LIMITED AND PRINTED IN HONG KONG

Contents

Gunpowder and Matchlocks

1 (*above*) The hero Roland in a Gothic tapestry surrounded by knights armed with different types of fifteenth-century weapons

'THE GUN IS AN instrument of death; choose it, therefore, for its beauty and precision'. This piece of parental advice would have been understood when it was originally given, in the eighteenth century, but it has lost its meaning today when firearms are utilitarian, mass-produced and barely decorated.

It was in the Middle Ages that crude cannon first appeared on the battle scene, but the principle of projecting

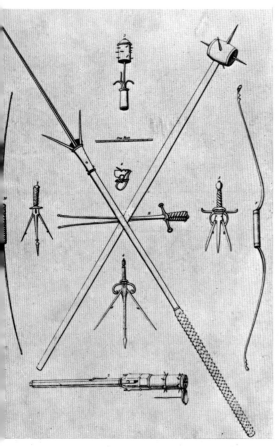

2 A trophy of arms, which includes a morning star as well as daggers with triple blades, from Meyrick's *Ancient Armour at Goodrich Park*

missiles was not then new. Since pre-history man had hunted animals swifter than himself, using a sling that propelled a piece of flint or stone, and by a more mature development of the same principle bows and arrows had later taken the place of the sling. Man relied on these weapons not only to help him to obtain food, but also to defend himself against his fellow men.

In the thirteenth century, before gunpowder was first used, the most important weapons were the lance, the sword and the battle mace. Pole arms were carried by retainers, and the knight, sitting on a horse arrayed like himself in plate armour, was protected from all these weapons. A stone or an arrow would have glanced off his armour, and it was only in close fighting that he might have been dismounted and mortally exposed. As further protection he wore chain mail beneath his armour which made him even less vulnerable. All over Europe the peasants were kept in surveillance by the feudal system, through which the lord of the manor or the king held complete power over his subjects. It seemed that nothing would change this system, in which armour was as symbolic of the immortality of feudalism as it was of the perfection of knighthood. Disputes between knights would be settled in single combat and armour was chosen regardless of expense, for its flexibility and resistance. During the fifteenth century the two most reputable armour centres were in Milan and in Landshut, a South German town; so that kings and noblemen in Spain, France and England had to go to the expense of importing their armour. It is not surprising therefore that there should have been much contemporary protest against cannon. It was thought monstrous that a peasant armed with a small cannon could inflict damage on a suit of armour which had been bought from the Missaglia workshops in Milan at great expense.

The history of firearms begins, naturally, with the invention of gunpowder, and there has been much controversy about its inventor and the date of his discovery.

Greek fire had been used against the Normans in the Third Crusade in 1190-91 and nineteenth-century writers assumed that this was the earliest form of gunpowder. This is not so. What was mistaken for gunpowder was an incendiary oil, which could only be extinguished by sand and not by water. Arrows and lumps of stone could be saturated in this liquid preparation and hurled from a great distance by siege catapults. Petroleum was an important

3 A portable combined three-barrelled cannon and battle mace, this morning star is known as 'Henry VIII's walking-staff'

ingredient but because Greek fire could be put out by vinegar and sand it could not have contained saltpetre, one of gunpowder's three major constituents. At first the European crusaders were terrified by Greek fire, but after a time it became clear to them that its effect was much less powerful than was at first supposed. Whereas it was impossible to see an approaching cannon ball, one could at least see Greek fire from a distance.

From the fifteenth century until the nineteenth century legend attributed the invention of gunpowder to an alchemist-monk called Berthold Schwartz. He was thought to have lived in the late thirteenth century, but, uncertain about his nationality, different chroniclers have described him as Danish, German or Greek. A statue was erected in his honour at Freiburg-im-Breisgau, giving the year 1353 as the date of his invention. But as Roger Bacon had written about gunpowder a century before this date the inscription was changed and Schwartz was credited with the invention of cannon.

The two greatest scientists of the Middle Ages were Albertus Magnus and Roger Bacon. Albertus Magnus, or Saint Albert the Great, was born in Bavaria around 1200. He entered the Dominican Order about the year 1230 and after giving up the Bishopric of Ratisbon in 1262, he devoted his life to teaching. A manuscript attributed to Magnus, *De Mirabilibus Mundi*, begins with discussions on magic. This is followed by several recipes for magic, including one for making chickens dance in a plate, after which come references to saltpetre. It is now thought that these were added afterwards. Roger Bacon, born in 1241 in Somerset, England, was perhaps more of a serious chemist than Magnus. While working with the Franciscan Order at Oxford, he wrote to Pope Clement IV asking him for permission to write a book, since to do so was prohibited by the Order. Bacon sent the manuscript of *Opus Majus* to Rome in 1268; the reference to gunpowder occurs in chapter ten of his book which is earlier than Magnus' *De Mirabilibus Mundi*. The legend of Berthold Schwartz persisted because Bacon, (who is now acknowledged to have been the discoverer of gunpowder), when describing his recipe in this work written between 1257 and 1265, wrote the formula in code, which was not deciphered until the nineteenth century. The English translation of the Latin text is, 'Notwithstanding, thou shalt take saltpetre, *Luro vopo vir can vtri*, and of sulphur, and by this

4 A fifteenth-century book illustration showing gunners as well as bowmen in a ship of war

5 The earliest known representation of a cannon that fired arrows is found in this manuscript of Walter de Milemete of 1326

means make it both to thunder and to lighten'. The words in italics form an anagram which, when re-arranged and re-spaced, discloses that the proportions are seven parts of saltpetre, five of charcoal and the same amount of sulphur.

The claim of Europe to be the Continent in which gunpowder was discovered has not been unquestioned. Travellers returning from the East in the seventeenth century reported that gunpowder had been in use in China before the birth of Christ, but they were probably confusing it with Chinese incendiaries and fireworks which were already in advance of anything in the West at the time Bacon was writing about gunpowder.

Like gunpowder the gun itself seems to have originated in the West. The earliest picture of a gun is in a manuscript dated 1326 showing a pear-shaped cannon which has just fired an arrow [figure 5]. The gunner holds to the touchhole what looks like a stick, but which is in fact a bar of red-hot iron. Rather crude portable cannon, known as 'crakys of war', are said to have been used by King Edward III against the Scots in the following year. But these early guns were not very effective [figure 7]. The process of refining gunpowder was not properly understood until the seventeenth century. Until then the three ingredients of gunpowder, (saltpetre, charcoal and sulphur) separated themselves in the process of being transported through being constantly shaken up, and on the field of battle the gunners had to remix the gunpowder

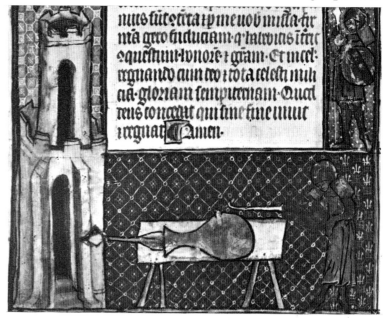

6 The medieval cannon, not readily transportable, was a more practical weapon during a prolonged siege

to obtain satisfactory results. In the seventeenth century gunpowder grains were mixed with a liquid into a paste, and when this cake-like substance was dry, it was broken down. The result of this was that the ingredients could not be separated, and the powder retained its potency. A further danger was that early guns were liable to burst; few men were prepared to face this danger, and in some cases convicts were released from prison for the purpose of loading and firing cannon. Detachments of men-at-arms guarded these unwilling gunners so that they could not escape, but this was found to be expensive and in the fifteenth century the gunner ignited his piece standing a short distance away, holding the match in the end of a special pike called a 'linstock' [figure 9]. Whether or not Edward III used cannon before the battle of Crécy in 1346 is open to speculation. Although the battle was decided by the English long bow, it is recorded that 'the English knights, taking with them the Black Prince, a body of wild Welshmen and many bombards, advanced to meet the French army ... they fired all the bombards at once and then the French began to flee'. This is probably

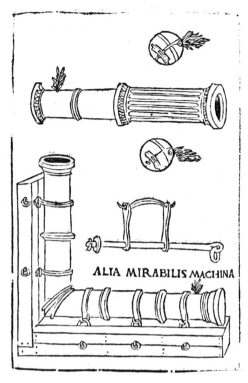

7 Valturio illustrates a shell and a curious cannon in his study of engines of war *c.* 1463

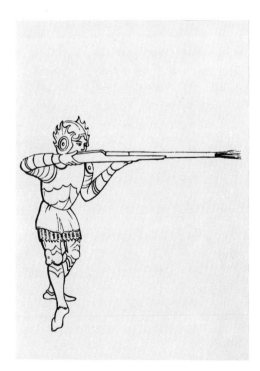

8 A nineteenth-century line engraving of a fifteenth-century manuscript, showing a soldier shooting with a 'handgonne'

an exaggeration, and what seems more likely is that the mercenary Genoese crossbowmen positioned in front of the French army were frightened by the noise of the cannon, and turning round tried to retreat through the line of knights whose horses were startled and confused.

The first 'hand gonne' appeared after Crécy. Similar in form to a small cannon and mounted on a block of wood, it was easily transported [figure 8]. This early piece could not be compared in effectiveness to the cross bow or long bow, but it had psychological advantages which were exploited by military strategists. The greatest limitation of the 'hand gonne' was that it could not be aimed with any degree of certainty. Held by the shooter under the arm or against the chest, the weapon required a free hand with which the shooter could apply a piece of lighted match to the touch-hole positioned on top of the barrel. So unsteady was the gun that it is hard to imagine it hitting a moving target, such as a knight in armour. Moreover the effective range of this weapon was no more than thirty feet. One needed iron nerves to wait until the knight was the distance of a lance away before one put a light to the gunpowder charge which might not ignite immediately.

A thoroughly welcome addition to the gun was the lock in its most elementary form: the matchlock consisted of an S-shaped bar which was pivoted in the middle, so that when the lower part was pulled, the upper arm holding the piece of lighted match in its jaws, would automatically come into contact with the pan of priming powder. This enabled the shooter to hold the gun with both hands and fire it with one finger.

The matchlock underwent several changes before it arrived at its most developed stage, when it was widely used as a service pattern gun, and remained almost unchanged until 1700. Although the flintlock, wheel lock and snaphaunce locks were fitted to better classes of firearms during the sixteenth and seventeenth centuries, the matchlock was retained for military purposes because it was comparatively cheap to produce. When loading, the musketeer first had to remove the match from the serpentine, and hold it in his left hand, well away from the powder while it was being poured from his flask into the muzzle of the piece. This charge would then be rammed down the barrel with a ram-rod, which for convenience was secured under the barrel, when not in use. A lead

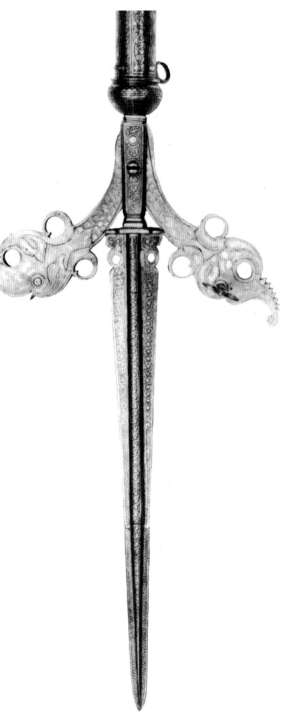

9 A late sixteenth-century German linstock with a matchlock pistol concealed in the blade

ball would then be rammed on top of the charge, the frizzen pan filled with priming powder from a smaller flask, and finally the match replaced in the serpentine. The powder for the main charge was a much coarser variety than the priming powder, and the two different types were kept in separate flasks. In the sixteenth century loading was accelerated with the introduction of the bandolier, which was a long belt worn over one shoulder, from which were suspended several wooden cartridge cases each containing the right amount of powder as well as the ball. In addition to the flasks and bandolier, the musketeer carried a forked rest, on which he supported the musket when discharging it [figure 14]. Sometimes it proved too difficult to keep a match alight in damp weather, so both ends were usually lit, but this constituted a danger in itself because during a campaign a lighted match might betray a position to the enemy.

The musket did not play an important part in the army until 1530, when Francis I introduced units of *arquebusiers* or matchlock musketeers into the French army. The distribution of these units among the pikemen was misjudged, and their services were wasted. The Spaniards, six years later, in a formation known as the *tercio*, corrected the balance by outnumbering the pikemen by *arquebusiers*. It took some time before it was realised that blocks of musketeers were wasted on the flanks, but by the middle of the sixteenth century when the long bow was entirely obsolete, they were moved to the front line where, protected by a thin line of pikemen, they proved more effective. The English attempted in 1627 to combine these two types of soldier into the London Company of Artillery by arming the pikemen with a shortened form of musket, which could be slung on their backs when not in use. The musket was in fact the more important of the two weapons and the rather bulky pike fell into disuse around the middle of the seventeenth century, with the increasing popularity of the plug bayonet, a type of dagger with a tapering hilt which could be pushed into the muzzle of a musket.

In the newly discovered colonies in America, the European settlers, particularly the Spaniards, found that both the crossbow and the matchlock were no match against the Indian long bow. One advantage of the matchlock, however, was that its noise, smoke and flame appeared to the Indians as magical, and, however inadequate in a

11

country simmering with hostile attacks, the matchlock was able to discourage and intimidate. But the Indians soon began to discover the weaknesses of this form of ignition, and even Henry Hudson himself experienced defeat after his men were caught with unlit matches in an Indian attack in 1609. Twenty years later a new type of lock arrived from Europe. This was a primitive form of the flintlock, the complexity of which prevented its general manufacture, so that the matchlock remained in use in the Americas until the beginning of the eighteenth century.

In the East, particularly in India and Japan, the matchlock was in use until the late nineteenth century. One of the earliest references to oriental firearms relates to Burma;

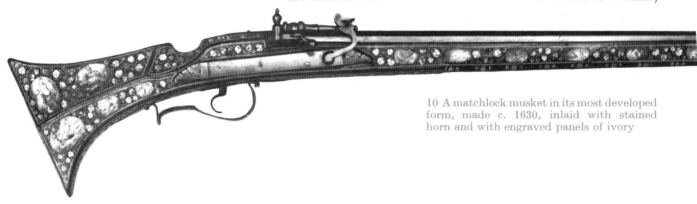

10 A matchlock musket in its most developed form, made *c.* 1630, inlaid with stained horn and with engraved panels of ivory

11 A German matchlock which dates from the late sixteenth century

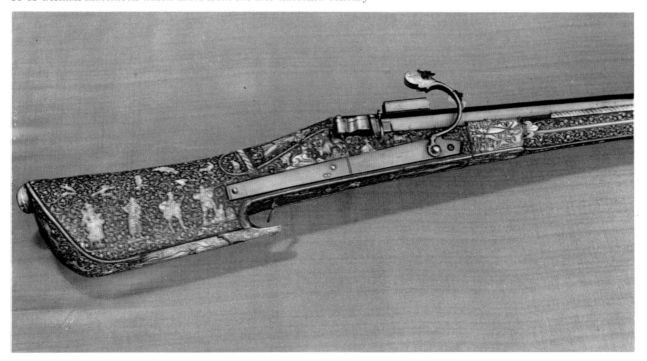

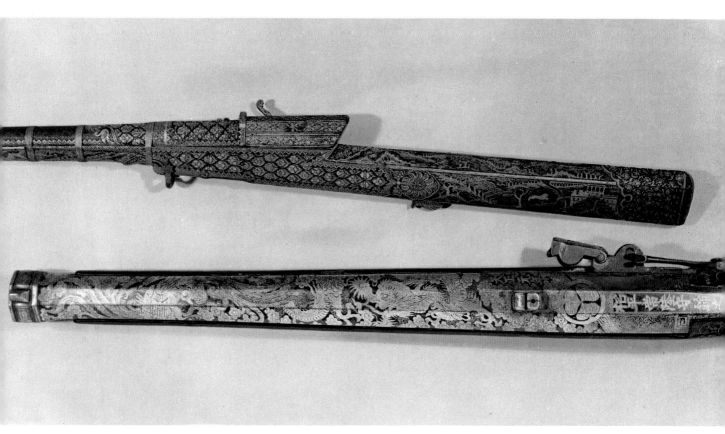

12 Oriental matchlocks: the gun painted with animals and foliage (*top*) is of Indian origin, made in the late eighteenth century; the Japanese matchlock (*bottom*) has a lacquered stock and silver inlaid russet barrel

13 An English shield and matchlock pistol, which was probably one of those carried by Henry VIII's bodyguard *c.* 1530–40

14 A matchlock musketeer of 1607, etched by De Gheyn, shown in the firing position with a bandolier slung round his shoulders

13

it occurs in an account of the King of Pegu's advance against King Meng Khoung in 1404 when it is recorded that the former did not dare attack the town of Prome because of the fierce bombardment from 'cannon and muskets'. This might, however, refer to rockets and fire arrows which were pieces of iron or copper hurled from a catapult after having been dipped in a petroleum solution similar to Greek fire, and then ignited. It is difficult to give a date to the introduction of the matchlock into India but it was probably about 1498, when Portuguese traders used Indian harbours as ports of call en route to Japan.

In the Orient the sword continued to be the most popular of weapons in spite of the fact that the wheel lock and flintlock must have been known from the Portuguese trading post at Nagasaki. These new types of lock were never in general circulation and although produced in relatively small numbers, the matchlock [figure 16] was improved to as near mechanical perfection as was possible before pin-fire ignition took over in the middle of the nineteenth century. On examining Japanese firearms one is aware of a brilliant colour scheme devised by their creators. In contrast to the brass locks the stock was often decorated in black lacquer, the finer pieces being enriched with gilt peony and lotus flowerheads. The russet iron barrels with their peculiar pod-shaped muzzles were inlaid with flowers in gold and silver.

The matchlock gained in popularity in India after the assault on Calicut by the Portuguese in 1510 when it was reported that the natives managed to repel the fierce musketry attack directed against them by setting fire to the city and showering the invaders with darts.

There was constant warfare between the different tribes and kingdoms in India during the seventeenth century, and the commanders of the various armies tried out novel methods of transporting musketeers. De Mandelsloe in his account of the Mogul army tells us that elephants were used to transport four or five men armed with muskets, but that the animals were so terrified by the noise of the explosion that this practice was given up as being totally ineffective. Bernier in his *Mogul Empire* (1658) has left us an account of the battle of Chambal river, when Dara went to the trouble of importing a gun carrier

14

15 A Japanese hunter in ivory holding a matchlock gun

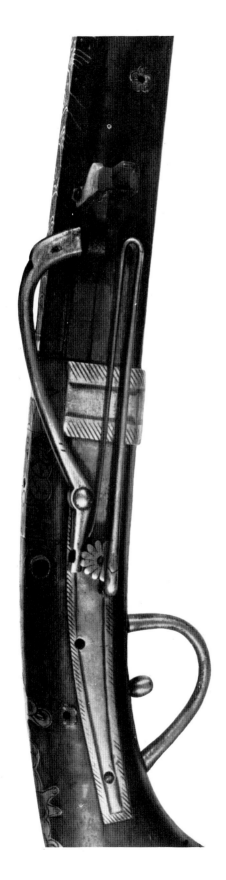

from Africa, which contributed to his defeat: 'Behind these pieces of cannon he placed a great number of light camels on the forepart of their bodies whereof they fasten a small piece the bigness of a double musket, a man sitting on the hind part of the camel being able to discharge without alighting' [figure 17]. But even with this new type of secret weapon Dara was overcome by the superior archery and skilled grenade throwing of the opposing army.

One would have thought, however, that in 1746, when the French and English armies were supporting different claimants to the throne of the Deccan, the European flintlock might have had greater influence on the firearms industry in India. But although detachments of Sepoys were armed with service pattern flintlock muskets, the matchlock prevailed in the native armies [figure 19]. If an Indian preferred the flintlock action, because the bore of an Indian gun is smaller than the Brown Bess musket and in order not to upset loading operations by having to cast larger bullets, he merely had the European lock fitted to his native matchlock. The native tribes in the north-west enjoyed a fine reputation as marksmen, and some are said to have shot accurately up to a range of eight hundred yards with their smooth-bored matchlocks, which is a feat hardly attained with the Brown Bess. It is not surprising that the Indians set great store by their barrels, for they were in most cases 'damascened', a technique of barrel construction named after Damascus, its founder city. Although Damascus enjoyed the reputation of manufacturing fine blades during the sixteenth century, the steel itself was obtained from India, and soon the natives of the latter country learnt the secret of steel tempering. The forging of a Damascus barrel sometimes took as long as two weeks and consequently only the better guns were fitted with this comparatively expensive type of barrel. While in Europe gun barrels were cast from one piece of iron, in the East bits of used iron were formed into ribbons the thickness of a man's finger, which were then twisted together. A further band was wound round this core and welded, after which it was again twisted and beaten into a cylindrical form and then bored. This method of knitting the metal produced a barrel which not only was unsurpassed in durability

16 A Japanese matchlock musket with brass lock fittings

17 (*above*) A dromedary, shown in an eighteenth-century print, waiting patiently until the swivel gun on its back is discharged

18 (*left*) A Chinaman shooting a twenty-shot gun from the manuscript Wu Pei Chih of 1628

19 Unlike the Japanese matchlock, its Indian counterpart had an enclosed lock, and the serpentine can only just be seen projecting from a slit above the lock plate

but also proved to be the most powerful influence on the construction of barrels in Europe during the eighteenth and nineteenth centuries. This technique was perfected gradually in India, and it was not until the eighteenth century that gunsmiths were able to prove the finished article by filling the entire barrel with gunpowder, being confident that it would not burst. Until then few guns would have survived a proof of a quarter of that amount.

The substance used in decoration was determined by the quality of the gun. Gold would be used for the lock plate, barrel bands and mounts of a presentation piece [figure 20], and in addition the barrel might be decorated with an intricate foliate trelliswork in gold inlay; this technique would be simulated in copper-gilt on guns of lesser quality. But the painting of guns, peculiar to India alone, is unsuited to the irregular area of the stock.

20 The Indian prince Akbar is shown in this seventeenth-century miniature holding a lacquered and gold-mounted matchlock

21 An early seventeenth-century print by Jacob de Gheyn showing a mounted soldier shooting a wheel lock gun

THE MATCHLOCK FORM OF ignition had had many limitations, for although in its last form it was a competent piece of mechanism, its performance was unpredictable in wet weather. What was needed was a more enclosed lock, where the spark would ignite the priming powder so quickly that the elements could not interfere.

The answer to this problem was the wheel lock. Tradition says that it was invented by a certain Johann Kiefuss of Nuremberg in 1517. However it is unlikely that this form of ignition was discovered outright, and Kiefuss probably got the idea from the spring-driven tinder lighter, which was then in common use. The earliest

17

form of the wheel lock is found in the so-called Monks Gun — a small cannon ignited by a piece of pyrites flint which was placed against the touchhole. A long roughened steel bar was held over this, and a ring was provided at one end so that it could be drawn quickly across the face of the flint so as to create a few sparks. This was extremely crude and the motion of drawing back the bar must have made it impossible for the shooter to aim accurately. But even before this, among his sketches of newfangled war machines and weapons drawn up in the *Codex Atlanticus* which dates from the last decade of the fifteenth century, Leonardo da Vinci included for his patron, the Duke of Milan, two drawings of a rather primitive wheel lock as well as new types of chain used in these locks [figure 23].

22 Made in Italy *c.* 1525, this early wheel lock pistol has an external lock

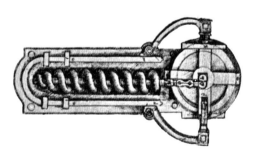

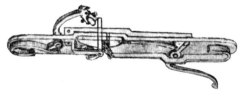

23 Sketches from Leonardo da Vinci's *Codex Atlanticus* in which designs for a crude form of wheel lock first appeared

In its earliest form the wheel lock was crude. Different parts of its mechanism can be seen in an early pistol which is probably of Italian origin, and dates from 1520-1530 [figure 22]. Sparks were obtained by holding a piece of pyrites flint in the jaws of the cock or 'dog' against a grooved wheel, which was rotated when the mainspring was released, drawing the multi-linked chain downwards. It was also possible to apply this form of ignition, which did not have to be operated manually, into a short hand-gun, or pistol, named after the Italian town of Pistoia, from whence it was thought to have originated. This particular example with its open action could not have operated well in bad weather, and the mechanism was soon enclosed behind a lock plate, and the dagger-shaped stock was enlarged so as to afford greater comfort to the shooter.

During the sixteenth century Germany and Austria monopolised the production of fine weapons in Europe, and it was not until the 1580's that they were challenged by rival manufactories which made their appearance in Italy and France. By 1540 the lock mechanism had been so

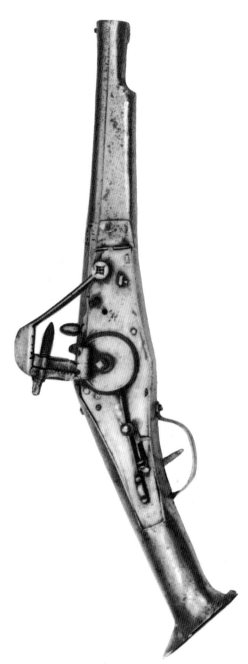

24 A German military wheel lock pistol
c. 1575, forged entirely out of steel

much improved that except for minor additions it remained unchanged for the next century [figure 24]. The lock plate sealed off the intricate mechanism from the elements, and even the wheel was protected by a cover. In later years craftsmen were to exercise their skill by piercing and engraving this cover which was usually cast in brass. The pan cover, whose main function was to keep the powder dry until the moment of firing, was automatically drawn back at the last moment. Up to the end of the century various shaped cock springs were tried; though crescent-shaped and curved springs were adopted, the V-shape one proved to be more reliable.

The intricate mechanism of the wheel lock made it very expensive to produce. Simple military wheel locks in England in 1659 cost anything between fifteen and eighteen shillings when a matchlock gun cost less than half that amount. Naturally it was impossible to equip a complete army with the more costly mechanism. Moreover, it was much easier to repair the lock mechanism of a matchlock; any blacksmith without specialist knowledge could join the stout pieces of metal together, whereas a broken wheel lock would need the expert knowledge of a locksmith or gunsmith.

Today the component parts of a gun are usually assembled as they are made. In the sixteenth century this was only possible for a very rich and successful gunmaker. On the Continent rivalries existed between the different guilds so that the barrel maker, who belonged to the blacksmiths' guild, and the lock maker who naturally was a member of his own guild, were not allowed to amalgamate. In England a union of these two took place, in the shape of the Gunmakers' Company in 1637; most Continental centres did not follow until long afterwards.

It is therefore safe to assume that the signature on a Continental gun made in the sixteenth century was that of the finisher who had bought the barrels, locks and stocks from their respective makers and had assembled them himself. Since the various dimensions of the locks and barrels determined the size and shape of the stock, the stockmaker quite often fulfilled both functions. German guns were not usually signed in full during this period; instead the three separate parts were stamped with their maker's own armourer's mark, thus continuing a tradition started by armourers one and a half centuries before.

By the middle of the century the pistol stock had become almost at right-angles to the butt-cap whose end was ball-shaped [figure 28]. In previous decades pistols had been forged out of metal, but now they were stocked in wood, a medium which provided much scope for decoration. Although by no means an elegant pistol, because of the bulbous butt, it did allow the horseman to get an excellent grip on it. Having developed the wheel lock

25 (*right*) A German gunsmith concealed a multi-barrelled wheel lock pistol beneath the face of this war hammer, made in the latter part of the sixteenth century

26 (*left*) In this early seventeenth-century colour print Stradanus shows Dutch sailors with matchlock muskets shooting camels to restock their ships

27 (*above*) The enamelled decoration of the gold Pasfield Jewel, made in the form of a wheel lock pistol, was seriously damaged by fire in 1817

28 (*above right*) The stock of this German wheel lock pistol is inlaid with designs in stained horn

29 An Italian all-steel early seventeenth-century powder flask

into a technically efficient arm, German stockmakers around 1560 started to make their arms look more attractive by executing designs of scrolling foliage and animals in ivory and stained horn inlay. Although somewhat over-decorated, the stock was relieved by the metal parts which were fire-blued. This process not only added a lustrous colour to the weapons but it also protected the metals against corrosion.

By this period the gun and pistol were considered works of art. Gentlemen began to wear belt pistols, and delighted in their decoration. Germany's export trade flourished, and in many English portraits executed in the 1570's the subjects are depicted holding wheel lock pistols which are obviously German in character. Jewellers were attracted by this fashion, and although few pieces of jewellery in the form of guns have survived, the Pasfield Jewel, is representative of the style of this period [figure 27].

Arms had to be smuggled from Germany into England via the Spanish Netherlands from 1560 up to the time of the Spanish Armada in 1588. Burgon in his *Life and Times of Sir Thomas Gresham* records that the chief smuggler was Sir Thomas Gresham himself, founder of the Royal Exchange in London, who had to ship these contraband goods to the Tower of London under the guise of silks, satins and velvets. 'You shall understand,' wrote Gresham, 'that every piece of doble geyne velvet is one thousand weight of corrin powdry (corn powder). You must devyse some waye whereby the things may be secretly conveyed to the Tower. If it is discovered (at Antwerp) there is nothing short of death with the searcher and with him who enters in the custom house'. In one shipment he is reported to have smuggled over fifteen thousand handguns and eighteen thousand 'dagges' (a type of pistol). As well as gunpowder and shot, the English navy was equipped with musket arrows. In 1593 the famous sailor, Sir Richard Hawkins, remarked that they were used against the

Spaniards 'with singular effect and execution, as our enemies confessed; for the upper work of their shippes being musket proofe, in all places they passed through both sides with facilite, and wrought extraordinary disasters'. The Spanish captured several muskets together with their arrows, but not knowing how to load them they regarded them with suspicion and discarded them.

It was indeed fortunate that the English were able to import guns from Germany because by the time of the Armada, the Spanish gunmaking industry was well established. Charles V, who as Holy Roman Emperor ruled over both Spain and Austria, invited the brothers Marquarte to transfer their workshops from Augsburg to Madrid in 1530. Since they had been two of the most outstanding gunsmiths in Augsburg, at that time one of the leading factories in Europe, they took with them an unsurpassed knowledge of firearms production. Although the first guns they made in a foreign country were Germanic, their surroundings were made manifest in their work, and a Spanish style emerged. In comparison with their German armaments their production in Spain was small and no firearms were made for export. The Spanish firearms industry did not come into its own until early in the seventeenth century when it began to manufacture the Miquelet lock, a simpler and better piece of mechanism than the wheel lock, which was really a type of flint lock.

This new-found interest of Electors and Kings in firearms in Germany brought about a demand for fine guns and pistols in the late sixteenth century. The gunsmiths and stockmakers who knew how to 'finish' their work competently handed them over to specialist decorators. In this way firearms could be decorated with designs taken from the latest and most fashionable pattern book. In Europe nearly all ornament was derived from pattern books published by the different engravers, except in provincial towns where the local styles of decoration predominated. In Nuremberg and Augsburg engravings for the metal parts of the gun were mostly drawn from the publications of Jost Amman or Virgil Solis. At first these appeared as a series of engravings to be used by any metal worker, but gunmakers had difficulty in applying them to the irregular shapes of gun mounts, with the result that engravers published designs exclusively for guns. As the century progressed, the shape of the stock changed and it became more flared. In the inlay craftsmen repeated

30 This typical early seventeenth-century Italian all steel powder flask has a lock key and screw driver built in to facilitate loading

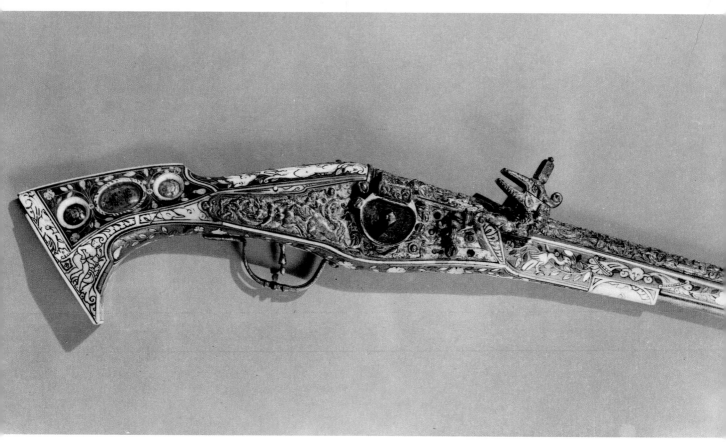

31 A French late sixteenth-century wheel lock petronel which is set with *verre englomise* plaques in addition to the intricate horn and stained ivory inlay

the patterns of flowers and grotesques designed by Adrien Collaert.

Undoubtedly the most important school of decorators was at Munich. Here from 1580 steel chisellers of the highest order, the brothers Daniel and Emanuel Sadeler, together with their successor Caspar Spät, continued to work for the Dukes of Bavaria for almost a century. They did not only confine their art to the metal furniture on firearms, but decorated such things as sword hilts, purse mounts and buckles. Unlike the other schools, the Sadelers drew their ornament from the engravings of Étienne Delaune, whose works were published in Paris in 1580. Their most typical decoration consists of figures surrounded by sprays of foliage chiselled in relief against a gilded ground. Respecting the very difficult nature of this work, steel had to be chiselled while cold. To set off these elaborate mounts to best advantage the stockmaker Hieronymus Borstorffer often made plain ivory stocks, enriched perhaps with ebony lines or light scrolls [figure 32].

Munich was the first German school to turn towards Paris for decorative inspiration. While other German gun-

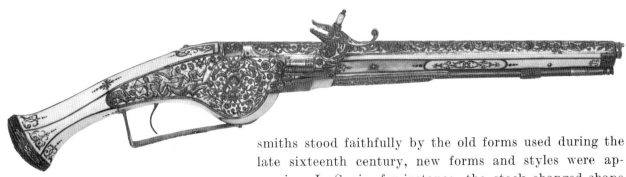

smiths stood faithfully by the old forms used during the late sixteenth century, new forms and styles were appearing. In Spain, for instance, the stock changed shape so that instead of being fired from the chest, the sporting gun could be fired from the shoulder. Advances in the refining of gunpowder had made this possible. With a more powerful and compact type of powder it was possible to make the barrel lighter and shorter. The German arquebus took all the recoil in its weight, but Germany was the last country to be reconciled with the new form.

Henri IV must be credited with the establishment of national workshops in the Louvre. A gun industry had grown up some twenty years earlier in the 1580's when a few extremely fine guns had been made. One of the most elaborate guns ever to have been made belongs to this period. A petronel (a short carbine or long pistol) dated

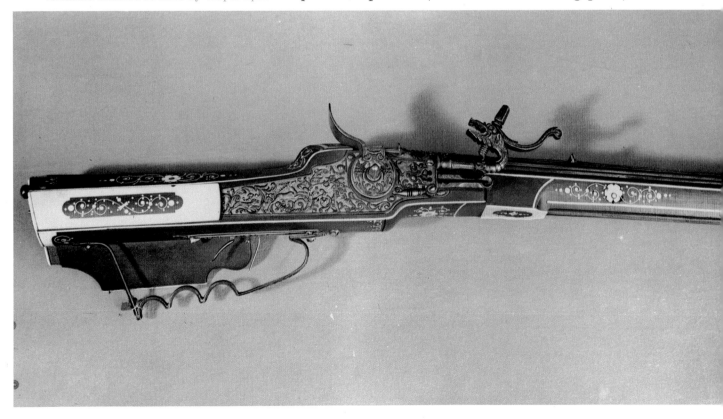

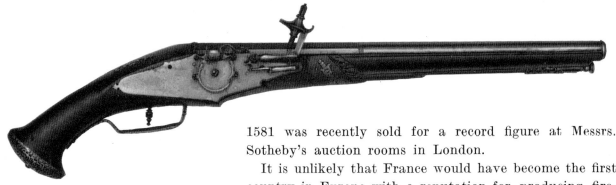

34 An Italian seventeenth-century wheel lock holster pistol with pierced butt cap

1581 was recently sold for a record figure at Messrs. Sotheby's auction rooms in London.

It is unlikely that France would have become the first country in Europe with a reputation for producing firearms during the seventeenth century if it had not been for the patronage of Louis XIII. From his youth he had been interested in firearms and one of his amusements was to retire to his gunroom where he had amassed a collection of sixteenth-century guns, and there to strip and clean his own 'birding' guns. When comparing a fowling piece made for him when he was seven years old to German guns of the same period, it is clear that the gunsmith had cast aside the intricately inlaid work in favour of an attractively polished stock with a gracefully flared butt. This set the fashion for the early seventeenth century, when France showed the rest of Europe the elegance of a plain wooden stock, polished to reveal the grain.

During the reign of his son, Louis XIV, an inventory was made of all the firearms in the Royal Collection. These were stamped with a number on the butt, and were removed to the armoury in Paris. There they stayed until the occupation of Paris by the Allies in 1813, when the English and Prussian governments confiscated the greater

35 The locksmith has chiselled the steel in relief where the surface is rounded on this detached Italian snaphaunce lock made c. 1660, but he has enriched the flat areas with engraving

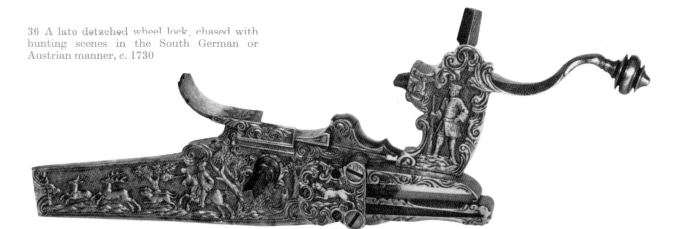

36 A lato detached wheel lock, chased with hunting scenes in the South German or Austrian manner, *c.* 1730

part of them and took them to their respective countries.

The popularity of the wheel lock was very short-lived in France; by 1620 it had been superseded by the flintlock which was less expensive to produce and much simpler to manipulate.

Armour centres such as Milan and Turin had been producing fine suits of armour since the fifteenth century, but except for a few wheel lock arms made in the early part of the sixteenth century the firearms centres in Italy did not get under way properly until the third quarter of the century. Gunmaking found its natural centre in Brescia, near which families of gunmakers settled. Adopting the South German type of wheel lock [figure 36], the craftsmen soon established a lucrative export trade with the rest of Europe because of the exquisite way in which they chiselled the mounts in high relief.

Dominating the scene was the Comminazzo family. Their barrels became so famous in Europe that pistols of Levantine and Turkish make in the eighteenth and nineteenth centuries were signed 'Lazarino Comminazzo'. Whereas north-European gunsmiths did not sign their names in full on their work, the Italians always did. Even so it seems unlikely that all the early seventeenth-century pistols which are in existence today and are signed with the name of this family could have come from the same workshop. It is possible, no doubt, that some unscrupulous barrel makers, like the Levantines and Turks, tried to sell their wares by signing them with a false but famous name. But it is more likely that the workshops in Brescia exported barrels in an unfinished state to finishers in other countries, and that these men engraved the signature on the barrels merely as a type of trade mark. It is curious that the best Brescian barrels are so thin that it seems

27

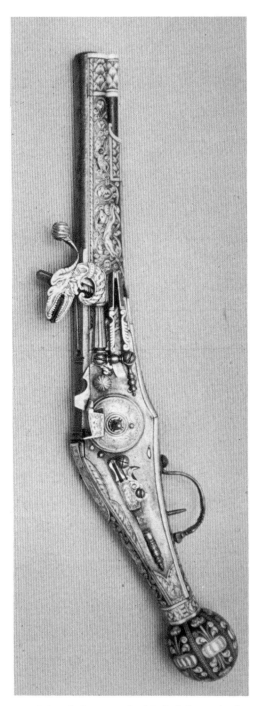

37a A South German wheel lock holster pistol, made for a boy, c. 1590

improbable that anything so finely fluted and decorated could ever withstand a blast of gunpowder. At first the mounts were finely pierced with tight designs of foliage, and the stocks were cut away behind them so as to provide a dark setting [figure 34]. This was given up in the middle of the seventeenth century in favour of chiselling in relief. The Italians, like the French, abandoned the wheel lock in the early seventeenth century. But they did not immediately adopt the flintlock which in France was still only in its infancy, and instead favoured the snaphaunce.

The word 'snaphaunce' comes from the Dutch, which translated means 'pecking fowl'. This is an apt description for this type of action which, in the majority of European countries except Germany, was the transition between wheel and flintlocks.

The action of the snaphaunce is a reversal of the wheel lock. Instead of the flint being laid on the steel which rotated, it was held in the jaws of a cock which was brought down on to a rough piece of steel, pivoted over the frizzen pan, thus causing the falling sparks to ignite the powder. The sliding pan cover was retained, but the scear engaged itself in the heel of the cock, and when the trigger was pulled, it was drawn back through the lockplate allowing the cock to fall. A half-cock safety device was considered quite unnecessary because the piece could be rendered harmless by raising the steel clear of the pan.

The snaphaunce first appeared around 1570 and enjoyed a certain popularity in the northern European countries. As it was comparatively cheap to produce, the snaphaunce was fitted mainly to service arms in such countries as France and Holland, but found a more important position in Scotland and Scandinavia, and later in Italy [figure 35].

Scottish pistols at first glance look slightly Moorish. This is deceptive, and closer examination will reveal the Celtic characteristics of the ornament [figure 38]. Although the stock of the pistol underwent several changes in appearance in the era of the flintlock, it was at first fish-tail in form. The centre of the Scottish firearms industry was at Doune, but unfortunately most of the arms produced there were merely initialled and the names of the workmen are not all known. But it is fortunate that so many examples of Scottish firearms are in existence today, and this is because the metal parts were nearly all cast in brass which is less liable to corrode than steel.

Unfortunately this was not the case in England, where

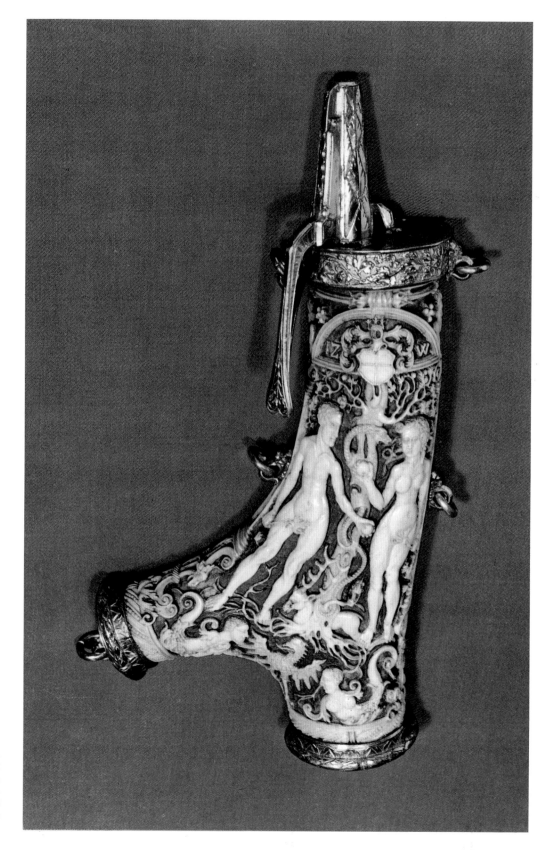

37 A sixteenth-century staghorn powder flask carved with Adam and Eve, and bearing the arms of a Tyrolean family

38 Slightly Moorish in appearance, this Scottish snaphaunce pistol made c. 1615 is easily recognizable by the Celtic devices engraved on the brass mounts and set into the stock

39 This elaborately inlaid chest was made in 1630 by Conrad Tornier, one of the most important seventeenth-century stockmakers

snaphaunce weapons are believed to have been produced in the last quarter of the sixteenth century. The practice of importing match and wheel locks from the Continent still continued, but evidence of an important national industry is given in the portrait of Captain Thomas Lee, dated 1594, in which the fine pistol he is shown holding is undoubtedly of English origin [figure 52]. The technique of encrusting russet iron with silver decoration was practised on rapier hilts and daggers of this period. Many of these have survived without their silver decoration; possibly this was stripped off when this type of ornament went out of fashion. King James I included firearms in his gifts to Tsar Boris Godunov in 1605, and to King Philip III of Spain a decade later; unfortunately in most cases only the barrels have survived.

By the time the snaphaunce was in use in Italy it had been developed into a very practical form of ignition. The chisellers took the opportunity to decorate the lock, which until now had been left rather plain. Masks were chiselled in the round at the end of the lockplate and the shape of the cock and steel gave them scope for the imaginative portrayal of figures and animals carved in the round.

German gunsmiths, who tended to ignore the technical advances made by gunsmiths of other nationalities, retained the wheel lock. But during this last period of its popularity in Germany, up to the early part of the eighteenth century, the lightening of the barrel allowed changes in the shape of the stock.

The ending of the Thirty Years' War in 1648 introduced a bleak period for the gunsmith who had enjoyed prosperity during this time, when arms of all description were greatly in demand. In Germany, as in other countries which had been ravaged, there was an unwillingness to invest money in fine weapons, and this led to the gradual disappearance of inlaid decoration. It is therefore rather surprising that one of the greatest stock decorators should emerge during this period. Cornad Tornier, an Alsatian, specialised in floral inlay work, using a vast range of coloured ivories and woods. His best work was done just before the middle of the century, and appears on both German and French stocks [figure 47]. Ironically, if he had not signed a richly inlaid box, now in the Wallace Collection in London, his name would be unknown to us [figure 40]. The series of stocks which he decorated in fact

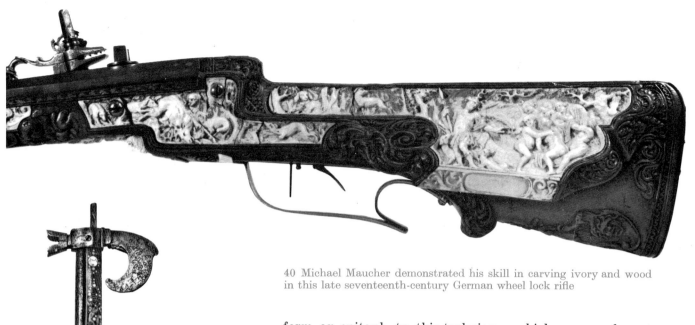

40 Michael Maucher demonstrated his skill in carving ivory and wood in this late seventeenth-century German wheel lock rifle

form an epitaph to this technique, which was no longer fashionable after the end of the Thirty Years' War.

Wood carving had been one of Germany's accomplishments since the fourteenth century. However successful this form of expression might be when applied to the interior decoration of churches, it proved unsuccessful when adopted by gunmakers. The Swabian carver Michael Maucher was the most outstanding craftsman in this school, but the shape of the stock does not lend itself to large panels of ivory carved with mythological figures [figure 40]. Although magnificently executed the total effect is one of effusion. Maucher's death just before the turn of the century coincided with a change to plain wooden stocks, enriched perhaps with wire inlay or carved with isolated scrolls in low relief.

In the Baltic provinces of Germany during the seventeenth century a strange type of wheel lock sporting rifle was in use. Known as a *Tschinke* it is easily recognisable by its exterior mainspring [figure 45].

Germany finally dispensed with the wheel lock in the early eighteenth century, by which time gunsmiths in every other country in Europe were experienced in the construction of the flintlock. It was almost a century earlier that the French had pioneered the development of its ignition, and had asserted themselves as the leading firearms manufacturing nation in Europe, a position which was to be seriously challenged when England became prosperous in the eighteenth century.

41 A Polish seventeenth-century combined axe and flintlock pistol

42 A French gunsmith's shop, *c.* 1660, bordered by gun ornament designs, listing several well known makers

IN THE EVOLUTION OF firearms it usually took some time for any new type of mechanism to be universally adopted. There was always a period of overlap. This is particularly noticeable during the first years of the flintlock, which as a form of ignition remained unrivalled for nearly two centuries. The flintlock was evolved in France *c.* 1612, and marked the beginning of the golden period of gunmaking in that country. Not until the 1620's did it gain currency in the rest of Europe when it was used in conjunction with the wheel lock and snaphaunce, and did not become the most popular of these locks until the second half of the century.

One of the results of the Thirty Years' War, owing to the

impoverished state of Europe, was a gradual decrease in commissions for fine arms. The effects of this slump are manifest in the restraint in ornamentation one detects on German guns, but even before this period France had dispensed with extravagant inlay on gunstocks in favour of extreme plainness, which proved to be just as attractive, especially when the graining was revealed by accomplished polishing. Because she would not adopt the flintlock in the seventeenth century, Germany yielded to France the foremost position she had held in the manufacturing of firearms during the previous century.

Before tracing the evolution of the flintlock it is perhaps instructive to describe two regional types of flintlock, the common flintlock in use in the North, and the Miquelet or Mediterranean lock. The first was in use in France. This consisted of a cock which held a piece of flint in its jaws, which under the force of a mainspring fell against a steel cover set perpendicularly to the frizzen pan. This produced a spark which fell into the priming powder. The mainspring on this type was entirely enclosed. By placing a detached snaphaunce and flintlock side by side, the differences are immediately apparent. The steel and sliding pancover are quite separate in the former, but appear as an entity in the latter. The other form of flintlock was the miquelet; because it is peculiar to countries on the Mediterranean it is sometimes known as the Mediterranean lock [figure 43]. It was particularly popular in Spain and Southern Italy. Distinguishable by its exterior mainspring it is in other ways similar to its northern counterpart.

43 Its exterior mainspring and severe outline identify the miquelet lock, used in the Mediterranean countries' from the midseventeenth century until the nineteenth century

44 (*right*) A portable tree-camouflage for a wild fowler engraved by Mitelli in the early seventeenth century

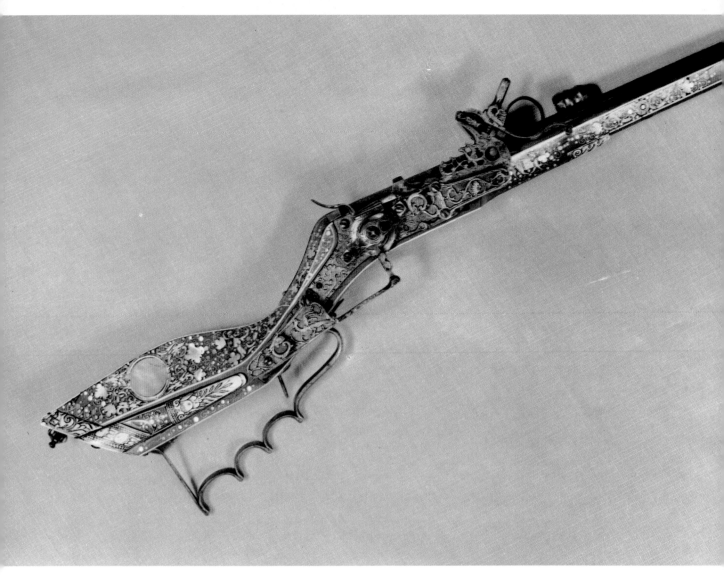

45 A type of wheel lock rifle with an exterior mainspring used in the Baltic provinces, known as a *Tschinke*

The earliest type of flintlock in France was equipped with a barrel-shaped pan, ending in an enlarged circular plate, known as a 'fence', which protected the shooter's hand from powder ash. This feature, although discarded in Europe by the middle of the seventeenth century remained unchanged in Arab guns up to the end of the last century. The first gunsmith of any importance in France was Marin le Bourgeoys, who was patented to the Louvre workshops in 1608 by King Henri IV. He, probably more than anyone else, was responsible for the early development of the flintlock in France, and fully appreciating the responsibilities of royal patronage set a fine example to his pupils and thus formed the centre of a promising national firearms industry. King Louis XIII's interest in firearms gave the

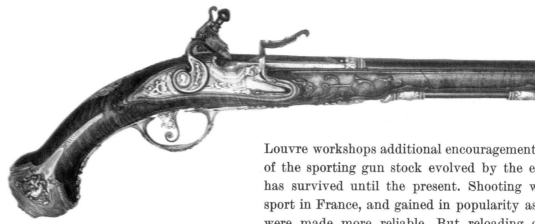

46 One of a pair of Italian flintlock holster pistols signed 'F. Bigoni in Brescia', first half of the eighteenth century

Louvre workshops additional encouragement, and the shape of the sporting gun stock evolved by the end of his reign has survived until the present. Shooting was a favourite sport in France, and gained in popularity as fowling pieces were made more reliable. But reloading after each shot was tiresome and the sportsman would have welcomed a multi-shot gun which would allow him greater freedom.

Multi-barrelled guns had been made by gunsmiths of the wheel lock era, but these had proved either too cumbersome or too dangerous to use, or else their owners were dissatisfied with the results. The demand for such a weapon was therefore partially satisfied when the double-barrelled fowling piece appeared with rotating barrels ignited by a single lock [figure 48]. It was safe to use, there being

47 An early flintlock gun with inlay work on the stock by Conrad Tornier

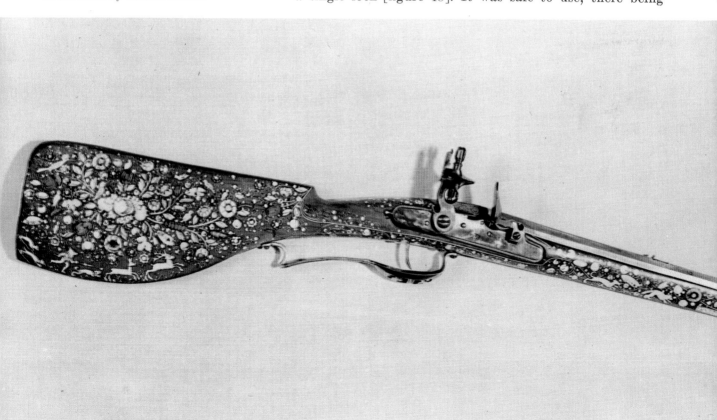

48 A double-barrelled fowling-piece with 'turn-over' barrels by Thuraine of Paris, who was one of the leading gunmakers in the late seventeenth century

only a short lapse of time between the firing of shots from both barrels. The sportsman merely had to turn over the barrels manually after the first barrel had been used. A spring catch was fitted so that the barrel was held tightly in position. This over-and-under principle when fitted to pistols remained popular until the middle of the nineteenth century.

French gunmaking reached its zenith during the reign of King Louis XIV. From the beginning of his reign in 1641 he was determined not only to regain the old frontiers lost in the Thirty Years' War, but also to make France the most powerful nation in Europe. To fulfil this ambition the young king accepted the advice of his chief minister Colbert who maintained that the first step towards this end was to nationalise all the industries. Money was poured into the armouries for decorative arms as well as for military weapons to equip the new army, and King Louis impressed the rulers of neighbouring countries by giving them expensive and lavish presents, frequently of pistols and guns. Thus designers and engravers were kept busy working on new forms of decoration. This period, which lasted from 1650 until the first years of the eighteenth century, can be divided stylistically into three parts. Around the middle of the century before Louis' new schemes were formulated, gunmounts were usually chiselled in relief, somewhat in the Southern Italian style. But the appearance of a pattern book published by a group of

49 A design for ornament on a flintlock gun from a pattern book by Philippe Daubigny in 1665; this very early type of flintlock is similar to the lock of the gun in figure 51

50 Classical decoration: *Le Roi Soleil* among trophies of arms on the barrel of an eighteenth-century fowling-piece

gunsmiths called '*Thuraine et le Hollandois*' revived line engraving [figure 49]. The subjects they particularly favoured were monsters recumbent in foliage, masks and grotesques. This gave a certain scope to the metal worker. Unfortunately this form of ornament did not require deep engraving so that few examples remain in their original condition, all traces having been rubbed off with continual handling. About this time a new metal piece appeared on the gun; this was the 'screw' or 'side plate'. Until then the screws which held the lock on to the stock had been countersunk into the wood. To make them even stronger the German gunsmiths in the sixteenth century had set them in an ivory or ebony washer. Now a piece of metal joined the two or three screw heads and provided yet another mount for the decorator.

The patterns of Thuraine were suitable in times of peace, but when Louis was engaged in endless warfare a more appropriate theme was needed, so new designs were made to celebrate triumph and victory. Classical motifs such as helmeted heroes surrounded by mythological figures or trophies of war now adorned good quality arms. King Louis himself was dressed as a hero, the gunmakers giving this motif more prominence by chiselling it in relief [figure 50]. It is therefore not surprising that this style, which represented France in the finest period of her history, should continue to be popular until the middle of the following century. Another series of designs, although not as appropriate for the decorating of guns as the Classical style, was introduced during this period, but enjoyed more popularity in other fields of art. These were by Jean Berain who propagated the application of geometrically patterned scroll and strapwork. Pirated editions of all these pattern books found their way to the corners of Europe, where they remained fashionable long after they had been discarded in the larger cities. Paris was the undisputed leader in the production of fine arms during the second half of the seventeenth century, but she left the production of military arms to the centres in North France. The towns of Sedan and Metz were the most important in this industrial belt and their gunsmiths often produced arms comparable to those made in Paris.

Many of these craftsmen were Huguenots, who up until 1685 enjoyed a measure of religious freedom. Then, much to the economic discomfort of France in the next century,

51 The Earl of Denbigh, the subject of this portrait attributed to Van Dyck, depicted holding an early form of flintlock fowling-piece

52 Evidence for the existence of an established English school of gunsmiths during the late sixteenth century is shown in this portrait of Captain Thomas Lee who holds a snaphaunce pistol of undoubted English origin

54 The Italian miquelet lock can be distinguished from its Spanish counterpart by the positioning of the mainspring as well as by the style of decoration

55 An unusual feature of this Spanish pistol made at Ripoll is the pad which protects the shooter's hand from the stiff mainspring

Louis revoked the Edict of Nantes, thus forcing them to leave the country. But if the provinces were impoverished, the countries to which the exiled Huguenots fled benefited from the dissemination of their art and craft.

Further north, in Holland, the firearms industries had prospered during the time of the Dutch wars with England. The town of Maastricht was the centre of munition supplies until it was sacked by the French armies under Louis XIV. But before this disaster occurred it had begun to produce highly decorative pistols with ivory stocks, the ball-butts attractively carved in the form of warriors' heads [figure 60].

Adopting the flintlock rather later than the rest of Europe Italy dispensed with the snaphaunce during the third quarter of the century. The town of Brescia in the northern part of Italy, well endowed with natural resources, held a monopoly over the smaller centres. As the century progressed steel mounts pierced with tracery were preferred to the old style, which still continued in Southern Italy. The kingdom of Naples, governed by Spain, had its own form of miquelet lock, which differed from its Spanish counterpart in the positioning of the mainspring [figure 54]. The Spaniards constructed the lock with both parts of the scear passing through the lock plate in front of the cock; these engaged a blade at the heel of the cock, with the mainspring passing underneath it. In the Italian version the mainspring rested on the toe of the cock, with the two parts of the scear positioned on both sides of it.

Simon Marquarte, son of the German gunsmith who had been brought over to Spain in the sixteenth century, is credited with the invention of the miquelet lock early in the seventeenth century. But even before this event took place, manufactories had sprung up in the Spanish provinces. Ripoll in Catalonia can be singled out as the most important centre, second only to Madrid, but such towns as Seville and Salamanca did not lag far behind.

Animosity between the two main centres caused their styles to be developed in opposition and therefore in contrast; Ripoll tended to follow a style very similar to that of Southern Italy, whereas Madrid was in greater sympathy with the Parisian style.

The heavy exterior mainspring, although allowing easy access in case of a break, made the miquelet lock rather stiff to operate. A large ring was placed on top of the cock so as to simplify the action of cocking, but it proved so impracticable that the shooting of rising birds was out of the question since the sportsman, after completing the action of drawing back the cock from the safety position, would find the bird out of range. Cabinets dating from the seventeenth century, made out of tortoiseshell and ivory, are often engraved with rabbit hunts. This was presumably one of the most popular sports, since shooting flying birds was almost out of the question. Compared with the northern lock, the miquelet was a very sturdy piece of mechanism and rarely misfired, but its stiffness of operation meant that Spanish exports were therefore limited to barrels. During the eighteenth century there was a great demand for these all over the Continent, and with the decline of France during the first part of the century, the Spaniards rose to a position in European gunmaking which was only overshadowed by the English.

It is indeed remarkable that English gunsmiths, who had learnt the art of gunmaking in the middle of the seventeenth century, should in less than a century be the most influential designers in Europe. The first group of gunsmiths had come over to England from the Continent just before the Civil War. Having enjoyed a period of prosperity during the Thirty Years' War, they left their countries when business was falling off and arrived in England at a time when arms were in great demand. The new Gunmakers' Company, founded in 1637, by imposing a gunpowder proof on all barrels, ensured that gunsmiths should conform to certain standards of safety. The barrels submitted to the Proof House were first of all viewed in the rough, and if the viewer was satisfied, a stamp with a crowned-V would be placed near the breech. The barrel would then be tested with a double charge, and providing that it survived this, the proof mark, which was GP interjoined and crowned, would be stamped next to the viewer's mark. Later in the century when cheaply produced barrels made on the Continent

56 A portrait of Prince Rupert, Count Palatine, attributed to Lely

41

57 A Brescian flintlock pistol signed Filipus Spinodus made in the second half of the seventeenth century

began to flood the English market, the proof mark acted as a type of trade mark and helped to sell the gun.

At the outbreak of the Civil War in 1642, the Royalist army found itself in a dilemma because London, with its trained bands and stores of arms, was in the hands of the Parliamentarians. However they were able to import arms from Holland, and officers who could afford it had their own 'screw-barrelled' pistols [figure 58]. Immigrant gunsmiths, such as Harman Barne [figure 59] began to produce these effective and advanced weapons, which were never made on the continent. They were breech-loading, and the barrel, shaped like a cannon, could be unscrewed so that the cavalryman could pour the gun-powder into a recessed compartment in the breech. The bullet was placed on top of this charge and the barrel re-screwed. The bullet could not roll down the barrel because it was cast just a fraction larger than the bore. This also helped it to bite into the grooves of the rifling as it was fired. The accuracy of this 'turn-off' pistol is illustrated by Plot in his *History of Staffordshire;* he records that when the Royalist army was resting at Staf-ford in the first year of the war, Prince Rupert showed his skill as a marksman by firing his pistol at the weather cock on the steeple of St Mary's church from a distance of about sixty paces from the base of the tower. His first shot hit the tail of the weathercock, and to prove to his uncle

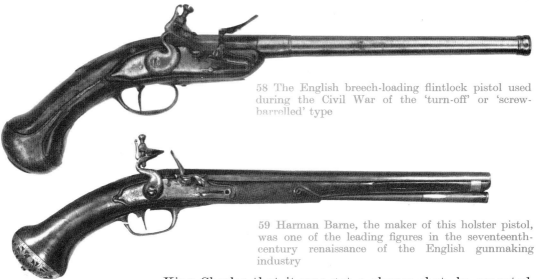

King Charles that it was not a chance shot, he repeated this feat. Armour afforded little protection against such a powerful pistol, and instead of wearing a full suit of armour, the troopers merely wore a breast plate which was meant to be bullet proof, a back plate which could withstand a sword thrust, and a helmet. Armourers impressed their customers by firing a bullet from a smooth bore pistol at the breast plate. This dented it rather badly, but did not actually pierce it.

Oliver Cromwell began the war with only a few trained militia men, but he soon enlisted gentlemen and peasants

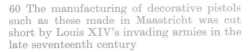

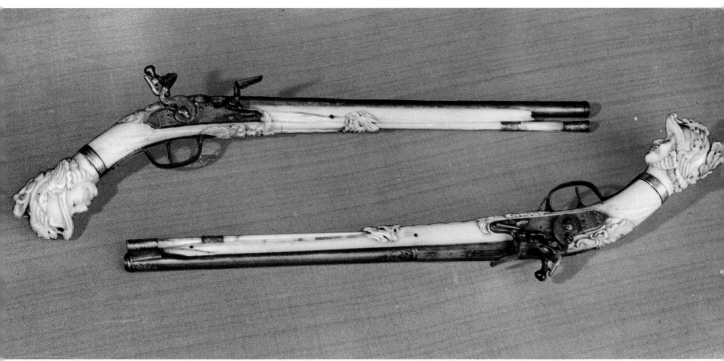

61 An eighteenth-century print showing two English sportsmen using flintlock fowling-pieces

from his own district, the fenlands. Shooting in the marshes was a common sport, and these men had learnt to handle guns from an early age. The Eastern Association (as his first troops were known) was equipped with matchlock or 'dog-lock' muskets, and its officers with rifled pistols. Putting uniforms on such men however did not really change them, and with hunters' cunning, they loaded their muskets with shot and used them as sporting guns. The officers had great difficulty in disciplining their men, who would shoot game at every opportunity in order to supplement their rations. But after all it was their last chance to hunt before it was banned under the Commonwealth. Serious target shooting as distinct from shooting for pleasure was allowed by the Puritan regime, and the old gunsmiths, who had few loyalties, continued to make weapons for Cromwell after the defeat of the Royalists.

While in exile the Cavaliers learnt several new sports. These included 'shooting flying' — a pastime they introduced into England at the Restoration in 1660, which more than anything else caused a renaissance in the gun-making industry. But the guns were not as good as the ones they had used in France, and as the gunpowder was still rather coarse, the sportsmen could not shoot at rising birds with much success. Because there was too much sulphur and charcoal in the composition, the mixture was sluggish and a long barrel was needed so that the charge should reach full strength before ejection from the muzzle. Added to this there was a noticeable time-lag between the moment the trigger was pulled and the charge was ignited. This was known as 'hanging fire'. Gentlemen, therefore, resorted to the unsportsmanlike habit of shoot-

62 John Cottington, alias Mul-sack, in the act of stealing an army pay-roll of twenty thousand pounds (from Captain Johnson's *General History of Highwaymen*)

ing pheasants and partridges on the boughs of a tree at almost point-blank range, after the birds had been pursued off the ground by dogs.

But firearms of such length [figure 61] would have been quite unsuitable for stage coach guards and naval boarding parties, when a large bore and handy weapon was needed. The gun which fulfilled these requirements was the blunderbuss [figure 63]. It appeared in England in the middle of the century, and takes its name from '*donderbuse*', a Dutch word, which translated means thunder box. This short fat gun, usually with a bell-mouthed brass

45

63 A flintlock blunderbuss made by E. North, *c.* 1760, with superior silver wire inlay in the butt

barrel, was a formidable weapon when loaded with lead slugs which fanned out quickly, and was lethal at close quarters.

Travelling in England at this time (as on the Continent) was very slow, due to the appalling condition of the roads, and few people travelled except of necessity. Travellers deployed over great spaces, unable to go at any great speed, were easy targets for highwaymen. One of the most famous of them was John Cottington, alias Mul-sack, who terrorised the roads of England under the Commonwealth and after the Restoration. He achieved his most spectacular robbery when he took twenty thousand pounds from a cart carrying the pay-roll from London to Oxford and Gloucester where some troops were billeted [figure 62]. A few years later he was compelled to flee the country, when he joined the King in exile. After a few months he returned and betrayed secrets to Cromwell in return for his freedom. He was pardoned, and carried on his profitable activities until 1685 when he was hanged. A blunderbuss might have been an effective weapon with which to combat such robbers, but it was not made in any great quantity until the eighteenth century, when travelling was accelerated.

Gunsmiths, since the inception of their industry, had toyed with breech loading systems, and in the last years of the seventeenth century new Continental systems found

64 A pair of flintlock pistols by Chasteaux à Paris decorated so as to conform to the dictates of fashion in France in the mid-eighteenth century

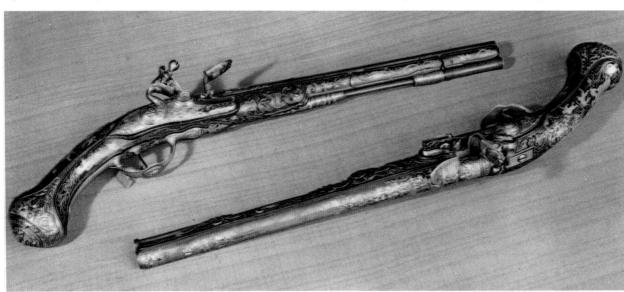

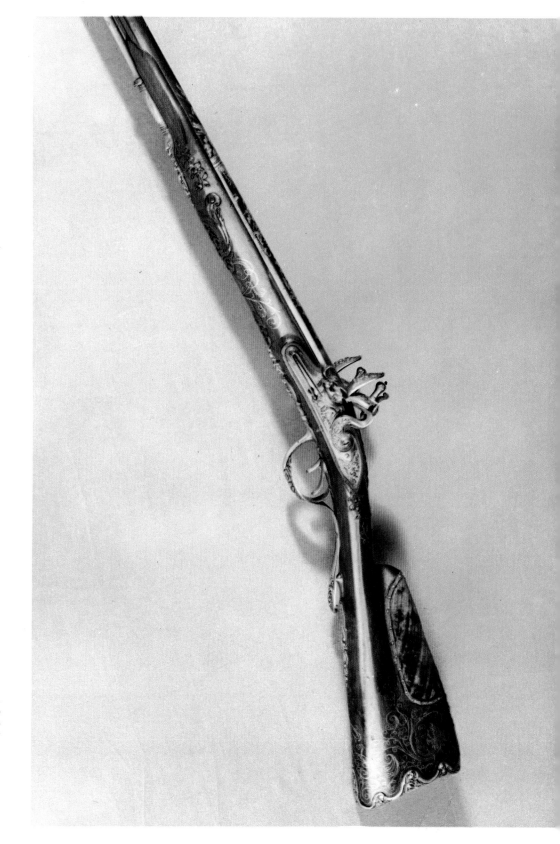

65 A double-barrelled flintlock fowling-piece made in France in the eighteenth century by Toupriant

66 The 'Queen Anne' cannon-barrelled pistol which achieved popularity in England during the first half of the eighteenth century (a previous owner added the ramrod pipes on this example)

67 The silver grotesque mask which formed the butt cap of English pistols of the 'Queen Anne' type

their way into England where they were developed with enthusiasm. It was difficult to apply the screw-barrel principle to anything larger than a horse pistol, and as a consequence various types of removable breech plugs were tried. But after a time the force of the explosion weakened the screw, and gas leaked through the defective parts — thus diminishing the strength of the bullet. Lorenzoni's magazine repeating system was introduced into England from Italy and was produced in limited numbers by John Cookson and Abraham Hill after the Restoration. This revolutionary type of action was applied to both pistols and guns. In this complicated piece of mechanism [figure 68], the charges of powder and ball were stored in the butt, in separate tubular compartments. To load such a weapon the revolving breech-block was rotated half a turn by means of a side lever. The gun, held muzzle downwards, admitted the individual charges into the recesses provided; this procedure was then reversed so that as the two recesses came into line with the breech the charges could be dropped into the chambered barrel one after the other. Simultaneously, the frizzen pan was automatically primed, and the cock set at half cock by a lever action attached to the breech block. Pepys had probably seen this gun when he noted in his diary on March 4, 1664 ... 'and then by coach to my lord Sandwich, with whom I spoke, walking a good while with him in his garden — there were several people by trying a new-fashion gun brought my Lord this morning, to shoot off often, one after another, without trouble or danger, very pretty'.

It is just as well that the magazine of gunpowder was separated from the breech by a rotating block, because if it had accidentally exploded the shooter would not have stood much chance of survival. Inevitably time loosened the breech-block, and rendered the gun impracticable; as a result early repeating arms are rare.

English pistols conformed to a pattern in the early eighteenth century. The 'Queen Anne' pistol, which was a smooth bore version of the screw-barrelled pistol used in the Civil War, was made in two sizes, belt and pocket, and was popular until the middle of the century when it was modified [figure 66]. It was breech loading and very simple to operate. An attractive addition which came in at the end of the seventeenth century was the casting of gun mounts in silver; all cannon-barrelled pistols being fitted with grotesque-mask butt-caps [figure 67]. Full

stocked holster pistols were made, but their design is more French in character. Barbar was perhaps the greatest individual gunsmith in England at this period, but many of his fowling pieces are fitted with imported Spanish barrels. The method of twisting the metal during the actual making of a barrel was best understood and practised by the gunmakers of Madrid and Ripoll, who had probably learnt about it from travellers returning from Persia. Their method was to melt down quantities of used horse-shoe nails, forge these into ribbons which were then wound round an iron core. The gaps were then welded and the whole polished.

The demand for weapons in wartime brought greater prosperity to the gun trade all over Europe, unless a factory had the misfortune to be situated near the scene of action, when, because of its military importance it was vulnerable. This factor was later to contribute to the decline of Ripoll, whose workshops, having survived two occupations and partial destruction in 1809 during the Peninsular War, were totally ruined by the French in 1813. After this date the town of Eiber became the second most important town in Spain.

The North African Arabs adopted both the snaphaunce and miquelet locks during the seventeenth century; the latter was constructed with a 'capstan head' cock screw. The stocks were carved with a very curving butt so that they could be tucked under one's arm whilst one was riding a camel. But gunmakers in these remote parts were technically years behind Spain and England, and it was in the latter country that the most important developments were to be made in the eighteenth century.

68 The arm on the left of the barrel enabled the breech block of John Cookson's flintlock magazine repeating rifle to rotate

69 A broadside illustrating the Puckle machine-gun of 1718; although not produced in any quantity, this pioneer design was favoured by American gunsmiths a century and a half later, when a reliable form of ignition made it more practical

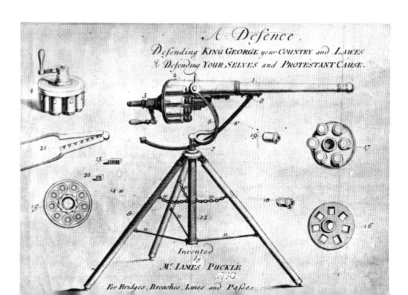

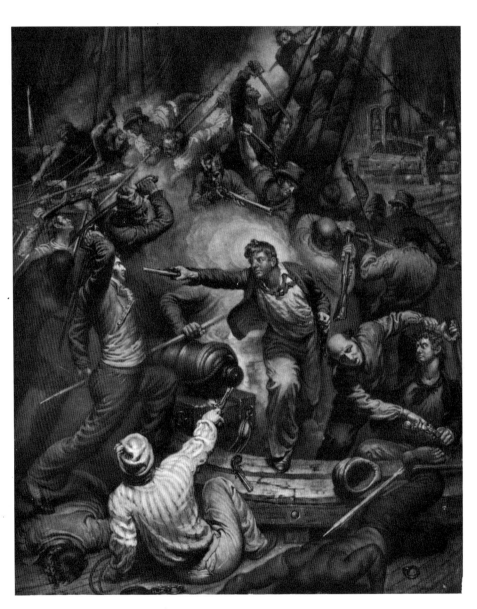

70 English sailors, boarding a Napoleonic man-o'-war, use their discharged pistols and blunderbusses as clubs

THE ASCENDANCY OF THE English firearms industry dates from Queen Anne's reign. This was made possible by the expansion in industry following the wars of the Spanish Succession and the accompanying period of prosperity. In Europe the situation was rather different. Marlborough, having used the Low Countries, Germany and Austria as a battleground, left these countries desolated and it was some time before they recovered. Prolonged fighting had,

71 In spite of a broken cock and a deeply scratched stock, this Brown Bess musket fitted with a grenade cup was still of use to a grenadier

of course, been expensive for England, but with world trade in the hands of her navy, and fleets of merchantmen, as well as expanding colonies abroad, she soon compensated for her losses. Thus the commercial middle class grew more prosperous, and, anxious to emulate the pastimes of the nobility, took up shooting. The gunmakers' order books were kept full.

In Prussia, too, gunsmiths were in business. There King Frederick William and his son Frederick the Great were striving to rebuild and equip the army, so that the gunsmiths in the Potsdam armouries, estabished in 1746, were kept busy producing service pattern arms. The result of their labours was spectacular. A decade later Prussia's newly equipped army was able to keep the French, Austrians and, in the early stages, the Russians at bay on three frontiers. Prussia's allies, the English, were armed at that time with the Brown Bess musket, which had made its appearance at the beginning of the century [figure 71]. It probably took its name from the acid brown barrel. Since this was the first standard size flintlock musket to be given to the English infantryman, detachments were given quantities of cartridges instead of bullet moulds and flasks. The Brown Bess was very popular and in the hands of an average shot, could fire about two or three rounds per minute — a vast improvement on the rate of firing by a matchlock musketeer. Colonel Hanger in *To all Sportsmen* (1814), said that the Brown Bess was accurate up to eighty yards, but that no one could aim at a man and kill him at two hundred yards.

Although affiliated to the British Army, the Highland Regiments of Scotland were allowed to retain their all-metal pistols. One can date these by the shape of the butt. The fishtail butted pistol survived until the middle of the seventeenth century, when it was followed c. 1640 by a lobed butt which in turn was succeeded by the heart-shaped butt. These were all produced until the middle of the eighteenth century. But around 1700 the 'ram's horn' butt came into fashion which is perhaps the best known of them all [figure 72]. The steel stock had an important function during battle. The form was for the Highland soldier to cover himself with his targe or small circular shield, run towards the enemy, discharge his musket and then drop it. After a few yards and at a distance of about ten yards from the enemy lines he fired and threw his pistol at his adversary; after that, provid-

72 A Scottish all-steel pistol with a 'ram's-horn' butt of the mid-eighteenth century

73 This Highland soldier of the Black Watch, who was shot at the Tower of London after the mutiny of 1743, is carrying numerous weapons, including a sockle bayonet strapped to his belt

ing he had not been hit, he attacked in close combat with broadsword and dirk. It is unlikely that officers, who highly prized their privately-owned pistols, decorated with silver and fine workmanship, followed this procedure.

Decoration of pistols at Doune, as we have seen the most important centre of the industry in Scotland during the eighteenth century, conformed to a type. Celtic ornament, consisting of scrolls and strapwork, was engraved on the barrels and stocks, or alternatively on silver plaques set in the stocks. The 'ram's horn' butt remained fashionable until the end of the century when the curved butt, then used in London, was adopted. Moreover, George IV's state visit to Scotland in 1822 brought about a Celtic revival, nourished by the novels of Scott; tartan became fashionable, and new designs were created for those who had no ancestral claim to wear it, in England as well as Scotland. Pistols had to be made to set off these new fashions and Birmingham produced a great number of 'Highland' pistols, which are easily recognisable by the poor quality of workmanship.

South of the border, in London, the cannon-barrelled pistol enjoyed popularity until the middle of the century. The most elaborately decorated arms of this period seem to have been made by immigrant craftsmen, although some English gunsmiths did attempt to decorate more extravagant pieces in the Continental manner. One of these, Robert Wilson of Birmingham, even made designs for a pattern book. But the market for pieces decorated with trophies of arms and portrait medallions in relief was very small in England, and the few gunsmiths who specialised in richly decorated arms exported the majority of these to the Near East, where such qualities were admired and paid for [figure 76].

The Germans had always regarded the flintlock with suspicion until it proved its superiority over the wheel lock early in the eighteenth century; only then did they

74 The grip of this Turkish flintlock pistol, overlaid with panels of silver, is smaller than its Western European counterpart

75 A typical Belgian all-steel pistol signed 'Segallas'

start producing flintlocks in any quantity. They adopted French styles in pistols and guns, but the manner in which they decorated mounts was derived from the Rococo. Compared with the earlier Baroque motifs, Rococo scrolls and designs allowed the gunsmith greater scope for improvisation. An example of the extent to which some gunsmiths improvised at this time is in a garniture in the Wallace Collection in London, made by the Stockmar

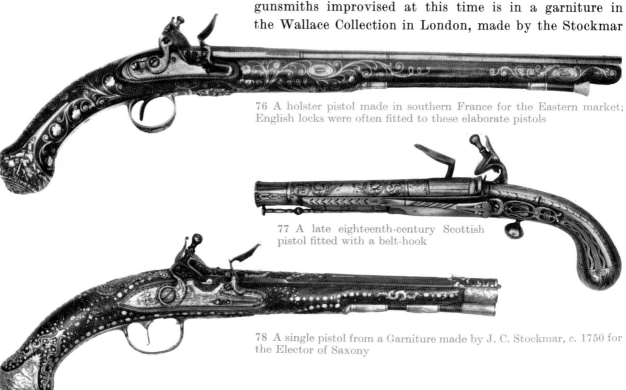

76 A holster pistol made in southern France for the Eastern market; English locks were often fitted to these elaborate pistols

77 A late eighteenth-century Scottish pistol fitted with a belt-hook

78 A single pistol from a Garniture made by J. C. Stockmar, c. 1750 for the Elector of Saxony

79 A Russian sporting gun made at Tula at the end of the eighteenth century

family for the Elector of Saxony, which over-reaches the bounds of fantasy and extravagance.

Many Liège-made guns in the eighteenth century are unsigned, or else are inscribed with fictitious signatures. This makes it very difficult to distinguish between French, Belgian and Dutch firearms. But the spurious signature most common to Belgian firearms appears on all-steel pocket pistols: that of 'Segellas' spelt in a variety of ways [figure 75]. Another give-away is when a piece made after 1810 is stamped with the Liège proof mark 'ELG'. Another group commonly called Levantine can easily be confused with Flemish pistols. Spurious signatures were put on these holster pistols by their Turkish or Near Eastern makers in order to sell them. Fantastic versions of London hallmarks also appear. However, the grip on the butt of nearly all Near Eastern firearms was generally smaller than it would have been in the West, and the shoulder of the butt was almost hunch-backed [figure 74]. A simulated ram-rod on these Levantine pieces also suggests a Near Eastern origin. In the late eighteenth century the Turks enriched the plain holster pistol by overlaying the barrels with silver muzzle bands. This continued well into the nineteenth century, and ironically this type of pistol was used not only by the Turks in the Greek War of Independence in 1824 but by the Greek army which had been equipped with English guns supplied by Lord Byron.

Russia had been one of the most backward countries in Europe until the accession of Peter the Great. Tsar Boris Godunov had started a foundry but it was not until a century later in 1705 that Peter the Great established a small arms factory at Tula. The iron ore came from the Urals, and although no Huguenot refugees appear to have gone there in 1685, Scandinavian, Swiss and Austrian craftsmen are known to have worked there after that time. Peter the Great originally intended Tula to produce service weapons, and by 1800 production was multiplied almost ten times since the year of its foundation, when it had produced eight thousand muskets. The Imperial Court also was a good customer, ordering fine arms either for its own use or for Royal presents. Before Tula was established in 1705, Russian-produced guns were of Eastern appearance, but by the mid-eighteenth century native craftsmen had learnt to accept the designs and methods introduced by immigrant gunsmiths. Like all craftsmen who are compelled to work according to foreign methods and designs, and

80 Blackbeard the Pirate, well armed with several brace of pistols (from Johnson's *General History of Highwaymen*); did he, in the event of a 'flash in the pan', ignite his pistols with his smouldering forelocks?

who are not fully acquainted with the techniques, their interpretation appears slightly clumsy. Tula made fewer fine guns after the death of the Empress Elizabeth in 1762 [figure 79], but continued to supply the army.

One must return from this brief international survey to England which during the second half of the eighteenth century was to become the focal point in world firearms production. London had, until then, monopolised the manufacturing of service arms, and when government contracts were exceptionally large, Birmingham gunsmiths had been sub-contracted to make component parts. But around 1775 Birmingham gunsmiths realised that if their guns could be sold by retailers in London under someone else's signature, they might with profit sell them under their own name. Guns labelled 'London' did command a better price, and with this in mind the London Gunmakers' Company in 1813 tried to get a Bill through Parliament forcing everyone to sign their work with the town of manufacture. The Birmingham gunsmiths took this as a personal attack and promptly set up their own Proof House, choosing the mark of crossed sceptres, crowned and with the letter BPC in the quartering. This gave Birmingham increased status, but her smiths, finding themselves unable to take over any business from the more fashionable London makers, continued to make quantities of cheaper weapons, such as Trade guns. These guns, painted an attractive pillar-box red, were shipped to Africa where they were traded for slaves by eighteenth-century merchants. Flints for these were being knapped in Devon for shipment to Kenya as late as 1930, where Trade guns were used by native hunting parties. Why so many were serviceable by then is puzzling because they were given only as tokens and not expected to endure constant use.

The last style to be fashionable before the English pistol and gun was stripped of all superfluous and non-functional decoration was the Rocaille. Its name was derived from its shell-like form, and was probably borrowed from Thomas Chippendale's designs for furniture and mirrors. Certain technical improvements were made around 1765 which enable one to date a pistol with accuracy. Whereas before this date the barrel had been pinned to the stock, it was now held with slides and secured at the breech by a hook which fitted into a 'false breech' which was positioned behind the proper breech, so as to quicken the process of dismantling it. Rifling has been referred to only in

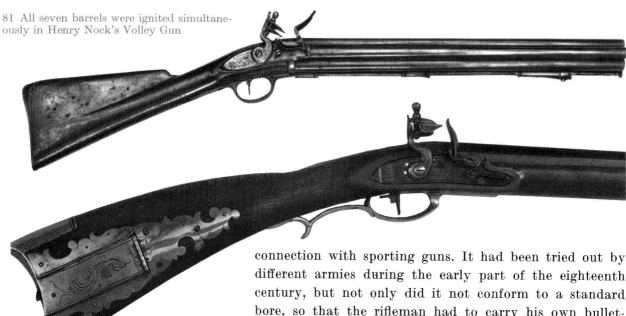

81 All seven barrels were ignited simultaneously in Henry Nock's Volley Gun

82 The butt of the American 'Kentucky' rifle is fitted with a trap for spare cartridges and wads

connection with sporting guns. It had been tried out by different armies during the early part of the eighteenth century, but not only did it not conform to a standard bore, so that the rifleman had to carry his own bullet-making tools, but also the smouldering remains of wadding left behind in the grooves sometimes caused a nasty accident when the next charge was inserted. (The English, who knew how easy it was to load a Brown Bess musket, scorned the rifleman who took double the time to load his piece and exerted twice the amount of energy ramming the bullet down the barrel. However, it only needed a series of defeats before the faithful Brown Bess was gradually withdrawn from service. This was to occur very soon afterwards.).

But in 1747, Benjamin Robins explained that deep grooves were not in fact really needed for a lead ball to be spun; shallow grooves would produce the same effect, and the difficulties previously referred to would quickly be overcome. The Germans and Swiss had already adopted this course in sporting weapons before 1710 when the first Germans crossed the Atlantic, settled in Pennsylvania, and amongst other things started to manufacture rifles.

These early Lancaster Valley and Kentucky rifles were long and thin and were loaded with bullets laid in greased linen patches, which increased the firing rate [figure 82]. At the same time the grooves were cleaned by the linen patch which had been propelled through the length of the barrel. The backwoodsmen soon became skilled with this new and efficient rifle, for in outlying districts their existence depended on its accuracy. In 1776 they were conscripted into the new American army to fight against the English, forming the backbone of this force. The British

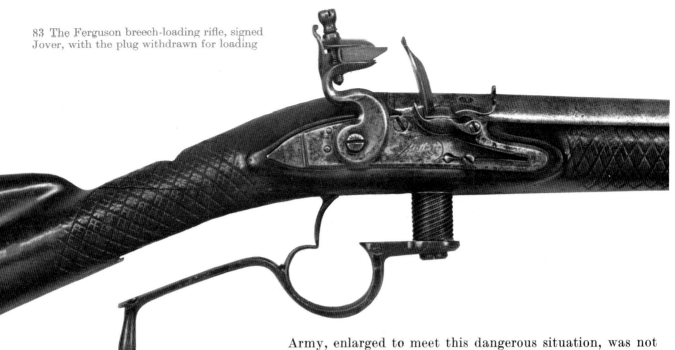

Army, enlarged to meet this dangerous situation, was not trained in guerilla warfare, for during the Seven Years' War there had been a pattern imposed on each battle and campaign. These fresh troops, instructed only in European tactics, were easily demoralised by the heavy losses resulting from sudden attacks in a rough and wooded country. A further disadvantage was the brilliant scarlet of their uniforms which could hardly be expected to blend with forest tones. Without camouflage they were sitting targets for the newly enlisted hunters.

Appreciating the difficulties they were up against, the British commanders tried various remedies. They discovered that armies of certain German States were equipped with rifles and eventually the Landgrave of Hesse was appointed to lend a regiment for the American War. But after money and time had been wasted in getting them to the New World these peasants armed with slow and heavy, ineffective rifles proved to be quite unavailing. One man who had control of the situation and was interested in the mechanics of firearms was Captain Patrick Ferguson, who had commanded a company of light infantry under the most adverse conditions and knew more about the situation than the politicians who ran the war from London. The rifle invented by Ferguson had two major advantages [figure 83]. It was a breech-loading weapon which could be loaded from a kneeling or lying position, and because of this the firing rate was greatly increased. His loading mechanism was a vastly improved

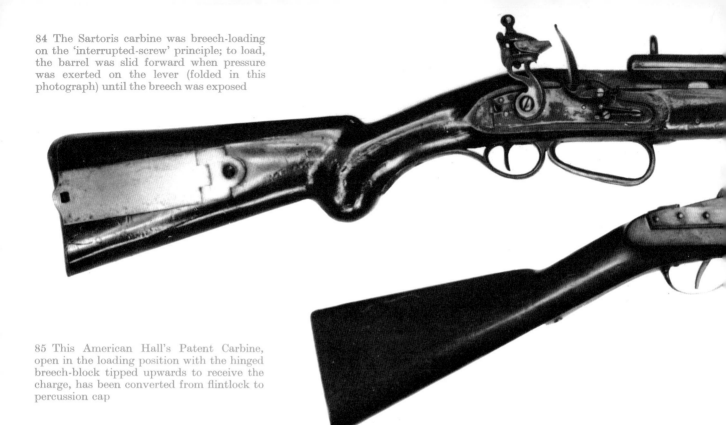

84 The Sartoris carbine was breech-loading on the 'interrupted-screw' principle; to load, the barrel was slid forward when pressure was exerted on the lever (folded in this photograph) until the breech was exposed

85 This American Hall's Patent Carbine, open in the loading position with the hinged breech-block tipped upwards to receive the charge, has been converted from flintlock to percussion cap

form of the detachable breech plug experimented with in the early part of the century by Bidet and Chaumette. Ferguson moved this plug to under the breech, the base of which formed the trigger-guard finial, the trigger-guard acting as a lever which, when swung three quarters of a turn, completely exposed the interior of the breech. Having completed this the rifleman would insert the bullet, drop the muzzle of the rifle slightly to allow the bullet to roll into the chamber and, after pouring the powder in behind it and re-screwing the plug, would prime the pan.

At his own expense Captain Ferguson armed and trained his men in the use of this rifle and in 1776 crossed the Atlantic when the rifle was used in active service for the first time. Before they embarked, Ferguson gave a demonstration at Woolwich in front of many high ranking officers including Lord Townshend, as well as several who were not convinced that the weapon was serviceable. In heavy rain he proved the excellence of his rifle by averaging four shots a minute, hitting the target with almost every shot at a distance of two hundred yards. Unfortunately three years later Ferguson, now a Major, was killed in a surprise raid by some Americans under the command of General Shelby. Whether out of jealousy, or because it

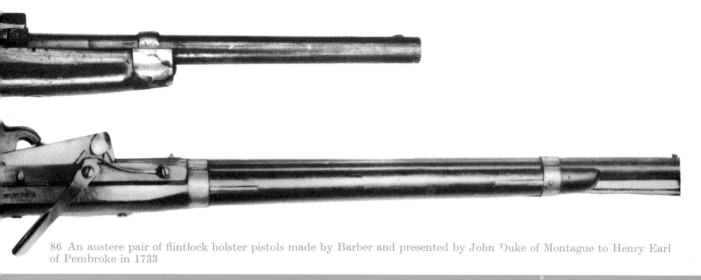

86 An austere pair of flintlock holster pistols made by Barber and presented by John Duke of Montague to Henry Earl of Pembroke in 1733

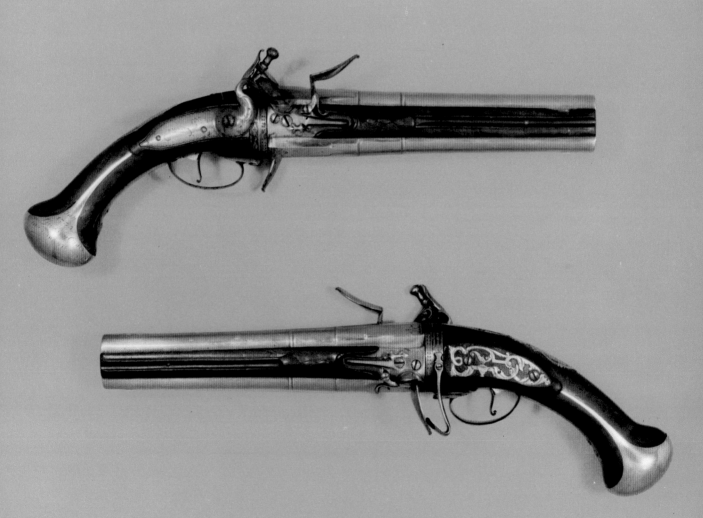

87 The formation of the famous 'Squares', which won the Battle of Waterloo, was still respected in 1854, as shown in this print of the Coldstream Guards

was considered too expensive a weapon, the Ferguson rifle was withdrawn after his death by the Board of Ordnance. But this did not prevent sportsmen in Europe from using it, or from ordering more lavishly-decorated Ferguson guns for their own private use.

After the fiasco of the American War, the Board of Ordnance held regular tests for new arms so that if they

In the later stages of the war various gunsmiths were experimenting with breech-loading systems. Tatham and Egg's rifle had a hinged breech which could be raised for loading. It was held in position by a transversal bar, but continuous use weakened it. Sartoris applied the same principle [figure 84] but joined the hinged breech to the barrel with an interrupted screw; to raise the breech the barrel had to be slid forward. The Americans were not long in issuing a breech-loading gun to their troops; stamped by the makers *S. North, Middltn, Conn* who were under contract to the American Government, it had been designed in 1811 by J. M. Hall of Portland [figure 85]. The breech-loading patents race continued well into the nineteenth century but meanwhile great advances in the development of the flint-lock pistol had been made around the end of the century, to which we must now turn.

were of use to the services, they could be adopted without

delay. In 1779 a seven-barrelled 'volley' gun was submitted for trial by an inventor called James Wilson. As a result of these tests Henry Nock, probably the most important gunsmith of the late eighteenth century, was asked to make twenty for the Navy, because they were thought to be useful in the 'tops' of a ship, from which position they would rake the decks of an opposing ship with deadly fire. But it must have been a very difficult weapon to re-load in a cramped crows-nest, and it was withdrawn from the Navy before Trafalgar: a fact that does much to discredit the popular theory that it was introduced into the Navy after Nelson had been killed by a sniper in the rigging of the *Redoubtable*. Nock's own invention, the screw-less enclosed lock, was also intended for use by the Navy, where lock screws easily corroded in the salt air. Although practical it was not produced in any numbers.

Nock's former apprentice, Ezekiel Baker, submitted a rifle to the Board of Ordnance test, which had a twist of only a quarter of a turn in the rifling. Out of many entries it was selected as the best rifle to go into production. Loaded with a patched bullet it was a great improvement on the Brown Bess then being used in the war against Napoleon, and contributed to the effectiveness of the squares at Waterloo, for, lined up in three rows, two-thirds of the soldiers had time to load their rifles while the remainder were firing a round. After the success of his rifle, Baker lost no time in writing a book called *Remarks on Rifle Guns*, which was very good publicity for him. Frequently in attendance on the Prince Regent, who was himself a gun collector, Baker published in his book copies of targets hit by his royal patron at Brighton. It is unlikely that the Prince would have been able to put three rifle bullets through the same hole, but Baker's flattery won him commissions to remount fine French barrels captured as trophies of war from Napoleon.

88 This example of an American 'cow horn', engraved with a view of New York and a map of the Hudson river, antedates the War of Independence by a few years

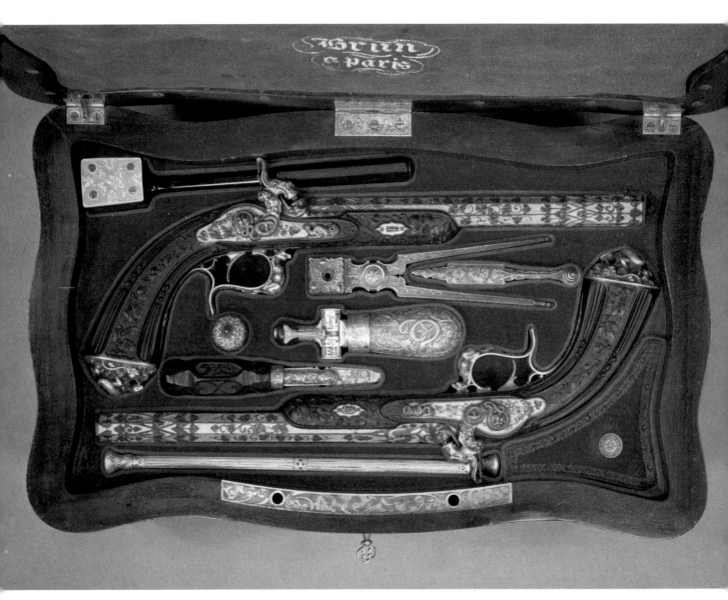

89 A pair of French 'Exhibition' percussion target pistols by Brun of Paris, c. 1845

FOR MOST PEOPLE 'the duel' is a vague, romantic concept, and few stop to consider at what period of duelling the sword gave way to the pistol. The rapier, which had been very popular during the seventeenth century, was superseded in the eighteenth century by the small sword, which combined the fighting ability of the rapier and the decorative qualities of the court sword. Conforming to the dictates of fashion, gentlemen wore the small sword as an indispensable part of their equipment, but many were unaware of its value as a defensive weapon and it was used with discretion. Fencing, however, was considered a desirable accomplishment, and when an Italian called Angelo established his fencing school in London in 1754 his large clientele included many famous figures of the time.

The pistol was used in conjunction with the sword in the mid-eighteenth century, the idea being that if a discharge were ineffective honour could still be satisfied by

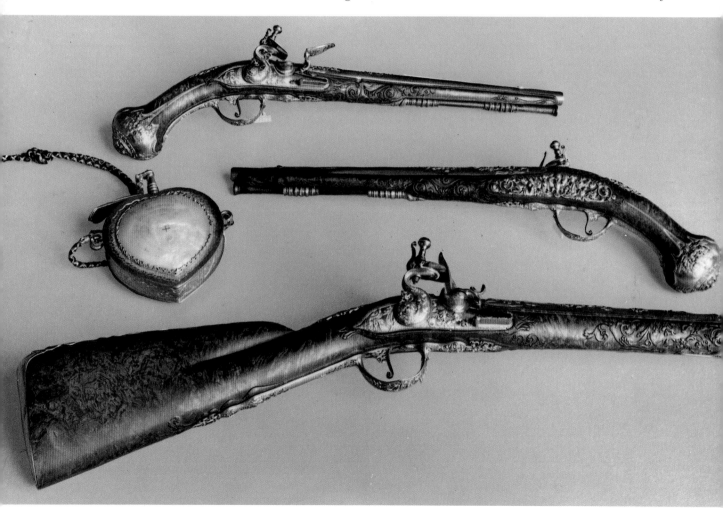

90 A mid-eighteenth-century Garniture consisting of a fowling-piece with its companion pistols and flask made by the German gunsmith Hermann Bougard

the skill and luck of the swordsman. And since a few lessons at the fencing school enabled a man to kill an untrained opponent with little difficulty, duelling with pistols was thought to be fairer. It admitted to a far greater degree the element of chance. Since duelling was never recognised as a legal means of settling a dispute,

63

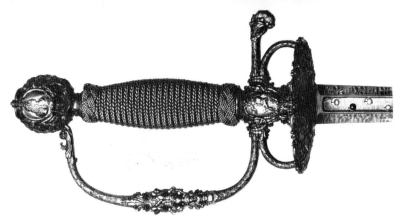

91 The hilt of a small sword, indispensable to a gentleman from *c.* 1660 until *c.* 1790

there was no universally accepted code; nevertheless there was a law against duelling, although it was never enforced until Victorian times. If a fatal duel were reported to a magistrate the free party could be charged with murder, therefore security measures were an important consideration and honour was best and most cautiously satisfied at dawn and in obscurity, so that the duellist who killed his man might be able to flee the country. Cased pistols of fine quality were beyond the means of most so that duelling became, at the end of the eighteenth century, the privilege of the wealthy.

Opponents authorised their seconds to make arrangements, more often than not elaborate, and to come to an agreement as to the choice of weapons and procedure. Procedure, though variable, conformed to the notion we have of a traditional duel. Standing back to back the opponents waited for a signal from one of their seconds, on which they walked the agreed number of paces, turned and fired. The paces were counted orally and the firing order given by one of the seconds. It was an offence to take deliberate aim. There were refinements: only one of the pistols was loaded, lots were drawn and action was at point blank range. Such procedures, however, were the exception, and were resorted to only when a professional duellist required encouragement to stand down.

The duelling pistol was a much modified version of the full-stocked holster pistol. In 1780, however, it was discovered that the silver mounts on an opponent's weapon caught the first rays of the sun and provided a target at which one instinctively aimed. Because of this, emphasis in design shifted from external embellishment to mechanical perfection and austerity of style. This led to one of the most significant developments in the history of English firearms, for whereas Continental manufacturers persisted

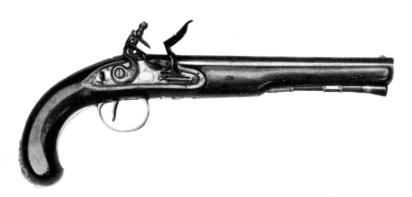

92 A typical duelling pistol, made by Wogdon
c. 1780; silver mounts were later discarded
because, by reflecting the light, they made
the duellist vulnerable

in copying traditional styles, English gunsmiths committed themselves to the realisation of mechanical perfection, which explained the undisputed reputation of English fire-arms up to the end of the nineteenth century. What bene-fited most from these experiments was the aged and ven-erable flintlock. The elimination of the side-plate was the most significant step taken in the development of the functional style. Shortly afterwards the spurred butt-cap was rendered superfluous; and, except on specially com-missioned presentation weapons, decoration was modest.

Opponents were forbidden to take deliberate aim — a difficulty that Wogdon, the gunsmith, tried to min-imize when he cut the stock of his pistol so that when it was brought up to the firing position it would form a pro-longation of the arm, and increase the chance of a fatal result [figure 92]. Wogdon's pairs of cased pistols were so famous between 1780-90 that the settlement of an argu-ment by duel was sometimes referred to as 'Wogdon's case'.

Around 1800 the chequered grip was introduced, a feature that was soon in demand since it gave one greater control over one's weapon. This was instituted by Joseph Manton, probably the greatest figure in English gun-making; he went further than his contemporaries by eliminating the butt-cap, and improving the mechanism of the lock. (When it is remembered how in the 1780's a roller bearing had been added to the frizzen spring to reduce friction — one of the first developments in gun-making for a hundred years — Manton's improvement will be seen as a rapid advance). He found that by stiffen-ing the main spring the cock did not have to be pulled back so far. This had the effect of speeding ignition. Furthermore he devised a V-shaped waterproof pan, and added a spur to the trigger guard by which the middle finger could help steady the pistol. An addition that was even more appreciated was when Manton set the fashion for barrels of greatly increased weight [figure 95].

The hair trigger which has already been noticed on the wheel-lock mechanism fitted to German sporting rifles, was simplified in the early nineteenth century, when it was discovered how one trigger could do the work of two. As the trigger was pushed forward a catch was engaged on a thin bar, held by a light spring which took all the pressure of the mainspring and scear in a very small

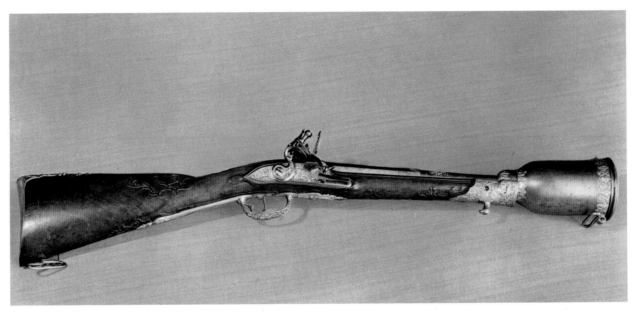

93 A German hunting rifle by Grafenstein à Gotha fitted with a grenade cup

detent. When this mechanism was set the slightest touch was enough to fire the pistol. A screw, placed next to the trigger itself regulated its pressure: if a duellist felt nervous the screw could be tightened: if confident — it could be released slightly.

In the eighteenth century pistols were bought by the brace. However with duelling pistols in such great demand gun retailers found it to their profit to combine both pistols with accessories such as powder flask, bullet mould, wad cutter, cleaning rod, etc. in a mahogany case lined with green baize [figure 98]. The pistols lay muzzle to butt surrounded by compartments for the smaller fittings. The maker usually pasted his trade label on the inside of the lid, fitting a hinged travelling handle on the outside.

So recurrent a feature is the duel in novels and films that one imagines it to have been unremarkable in eighteenth and nineteenth-century England. Since the practice was illegal it is difficult for us to form a numerical impression; and though public attention was drawn to duels

94 A somewhat lethal Bible: two Italian flintlock pistols were set into its covers in the early nineteenth century

fought by famous persons their action was nonetheless extreme. Above all, the duel was a strictly private means of settling a dispute in which fair play was ensured by one's friends.

A rather charming epitaph to what must have been a grim encounter is reported in the *Gentleman's Magazine*: 'Having first searched in each other's breasts for secret armour,' Sir James Stewart, Master of Blantyre, and Sir George Wharton 'fought a duel near Islington wherein they killed each other.' The report adds that 'When the king heard of this sad incident he was very sorry, and ordered them both to be buried in one grave' [figure 97]. One of the most famous duels took place nine years later between the Foreign Secretary, Mr Canning, and Lord Castlereagh who had launched a bitter personal attack against the former after the failure of the Walcheren Expedition. Both parties missed at the first exchange of shots, and their pistols were re-loaded. In the second exchange the Foreign Secretary was hit in the leg, and

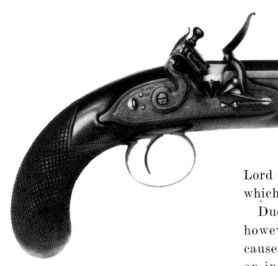

95 Designed by Joseph Manton *c.* 1815, this pistol has a heavy barrel and deeply carved grips to afford the duellist maximum comfort

96 Mortimer was one of the first gunmakers to give his guns a distinctive trade label.

Lord Castlereagh miraculously escaped death from a bullet which was deflected by one of his coat buttons.

Duels were sometimes fought for very trifling reasons, however. For example, a man was wounded in 1840 because of Lord Cardigan's aversion to undecanted claret, an incident known as the Black Bottle Affair. A Captain Reynolds was arrested for putting claret on a mess-table in a black bottle instead of a decanter. An account of this appeared in the *Morning Chronicle*, whereupon Cardigan challenged the writer, Captain Harvey Tuckett, to a duel. The Captain was wounded by the second shot, and Cardigan tried in the House of Lords, was declared not guilty. The fact that he was called on to justify his behaviour is indicative of the change in public attitude and the Victorian concern for the safeguard of its own respectability. After the Crimean War few duels are recorded.

In France after the Revolution men found that the guillotine and a secret service open to bribery were as efficient in eliminating opponents as a pair of Mantons. Thus there was less of a demand for fine weapons than in England. At the same time the guilds had been abolished during the reign of Louis XVI, with the result that the supply of apprentices and skilled craftsmen had also been radically reduced. The revolutionary government was quick to realise that production was too low, and in 1792 established a factory in the Grand Common of the palace at Versailles which was to be directed by Nicholas Noel Boutet. Boutet who was born in 1761, inherited the title of *Arquebusier du Roi* from his father-in-law, the gunmaker Desainte. Boutet, however, signed his work *Boutet Directeur Artiste Mannfure à Versailles* until the restoration of the Bourbons in 1816.

A year after he was made director Boutet was ordered to increase the craftsmen at Versailles by recruiting gunsmiths from Liège; and to renovate the equipment of his workshops. Not since Colbert had French firearms received such lavish consideration. Some of the most elaborate and generous presentation arms ever produced were made simultaneously with munitions for the wars. Boutet was able to design, execute and decorate his guns irrespective of economy. Although there was considerable variation in the quality of arms produced by Boutet, it must have been his genius for design and sculptural work that prompted Napoleon to grant him a monopoly of work at Versailles from 1800 until 1818.

Boutet's most successful pieces were decorated with motifs celebrating Napoleon's campaigns in Egypt. This style was an assimilation of sphinx, caryatid and anthemion motifs. Another attractive feature was the application of gilt stars on to a fire-blued barrel. Compared, however, with the simplicity of Manton's pistols, Boutet's were dressed to kill, and though he had benefited from certain English innovations such as the roller bearing on the frizzen spring and the set trigger, his lock was hardly comparable. His butt fell in the English manner — almost at right-angles, but instead of considering the enlarged butt-cap superfluous Boutet saw it as an excuse for even further decoration. Boutet's butt designs were emulated by other European gunsmiths until the middle of the century. A fashion adopted on the Continent (but hardly ever used in England) was for the fore-stock to be shortened into what was known as the half-stock. The swan-shaped cock which had remained almost unchanged until 1800 would obviously have been quite unsuitable for such a

97 An illustration from *The Gentleman's Magazine*, November 1800, commemorating the duel in Islington Fields which proved fatal to both parties

98 A case of pistols of *c.* 1815 with saw-handles and spur triggers designed to accommodate the fingers of a nervous duellist

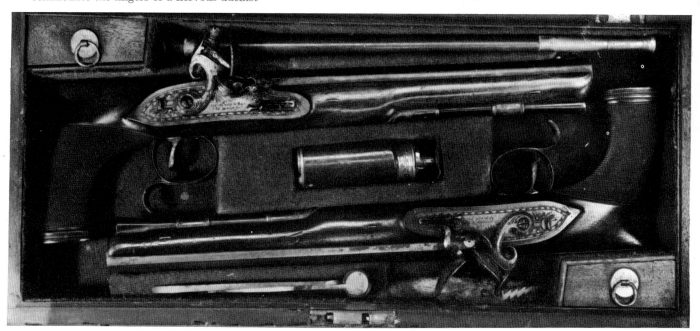

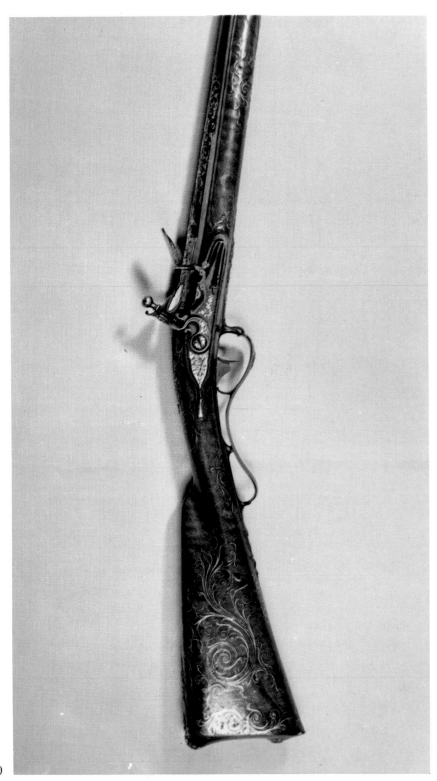

99 A Russian fowling-piece made at the armouries at Tula during the reign of the Empress Catherine

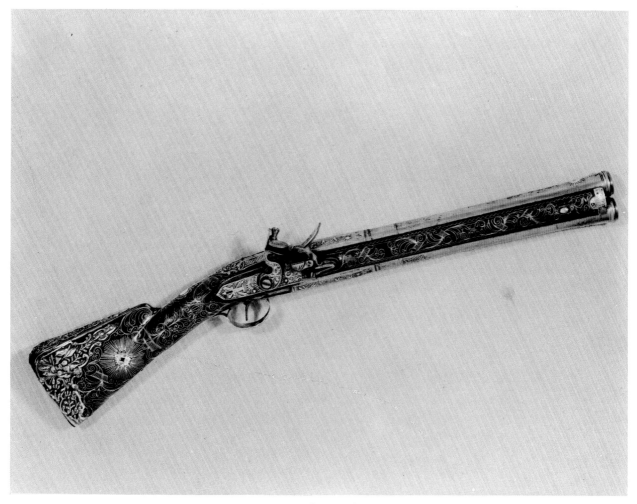

100 A rare example of a two-barrelled Turkish blunderbuss made in the early nineteenth century

square form of pistol, and on a flat lock plate. However, the new form, introduced by Boutet at the turn of the century, of tapering 'C'-scroll form, proved quite acceptable.

After Napoleon's defeat Paris and its environs were sacked, including the arms factory at Versailles. Boutet moved to the capital but never recovered from the downfall of his patron, the spoliation of his premises and the death of his eldest son. The fortunes of France were at their lowest ebb and most of Boutet's customers were either unable or reluctant to spend money on luxuries, and he consoled himself with a few foreign commissions, his international reputation still being a considerable one. An example of one of a pair of pistols made during this period for Lord Lynedoch is very English in character [figure 106]: the barrels are not blued but browned, the butt is cut in the round, not squared as in the Continental style; the rifling is multigrooved — a process considered extravagant

101 The force of the explosion propelled the wheel of this early nineteenth-century powder-tester so that a reading of its potency could be made on the gauge engraved on the rim

102 In 1799 Englishmen found themselves with numerous French opponents against whom they could match their skill at target shooting

by English makers since it took two men to make three grooves in one day, each groove having to be filed two thousand, five hundred times, and each barrel having ninety-two grooves. Lepage, the official gunmaker to Napoleon, was not as prolific in producing luxury arms as Boutet, the opulence and curiosity of whose pieces remind one of the golden age of Bavarian and Saxon arms.

Duelling is first heard of in America early in the nineteenth century. Laws relating to it differed from state to state; in some areas it was unknown, in others the guilty party had to forfeit any privileges of citizenship or public office that he might hold.

There was no set code, but in 1858 John Wilson summarised accepted behaviour in his *Code of Honor*.

'1 The arms used should be smooth-bore pistols, not exceeding nine inches in length, with flint and steel. Percussion pistols may be mutually used if agreed on, but to object on that account is lawful.

2 Each second informs the other when he is about to load, and invites his presence, but the seconds rarely attend on such invitation as gentlemen may be safely trusted in this matter.

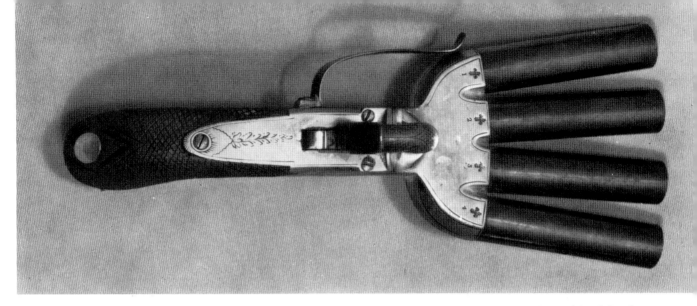

103 A 'duck's foot' or 'howdah' pistol, which proved an effective weapon for a sea captain when confronted by a mutinous crew

3   The second, in presenting the pistol to his friend, should never put it in his pistol hand, but should place it in the other, which is grasped midway along the barrel, with the muzzle pointing in the contrary way to that which he is to fire, informing him that his pistol is loaded and ready for use. Before the word is given, the principal grasps the butt firmly in his pistol hand, and brings it muzzle downward to the fighting position.

4   The fighting position is with the muzzle down and the barrel from you; for although it may be agreed that you may hold your pistol with the muzzle up, it may be objected to, as you can fire sooner from that position, and consequently have a decided advantage, which might not be claimed, and should not be granted.'

It seems rather incongruous that these rules should have been drawn up when both the percussion cap pistol and revolver were already in general use. Duels with the latter were not unheard of; they were used, for example, in the rather barbaric 'duel at a stalk', when both parties, provided with six-shot revolvers, stalked each other over a rocky terrain. A more civilized form was for opponents to face at a considerable distance and walk towards each other. It must have been tempting to fire several long shots in the hope that one might prove fatal; the winner, however, was usually the one who saved all six shots until his opponent was well within range. Perhaps Wilson's publication was an attempt to eradicate this particular method and so raise the status of the duel as a gentlemanly means to an honourable ending.

In 1830 James Sega in *The Means to Suppress the Practice*

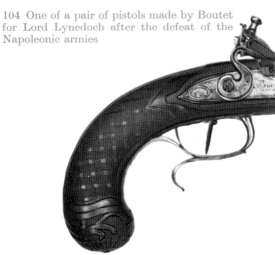

104 One of a pair of pistols made by Boutet for Lord Lynedoch after the defeat of the Napoleonic armies

105 A silver-barrelled pistol made in the Lucknow Arsenal in India in the late eighteenth century

of Duelling, asked 'Why does not the law punish in the like manner him who seduces another's wife, or betrays the daughter of a loving father? Is it that wives and daughters are not as valuable a possession as money, among civilized people? No husband, no father will challenge him, who, being imprisoned, belongs no longer to society'. However, it does not appear that any notice was taken of Mr Sega's recommendations and no legislation followed, but duelling was becoming obsolete. After the Civil War duels were infrequent and rare.

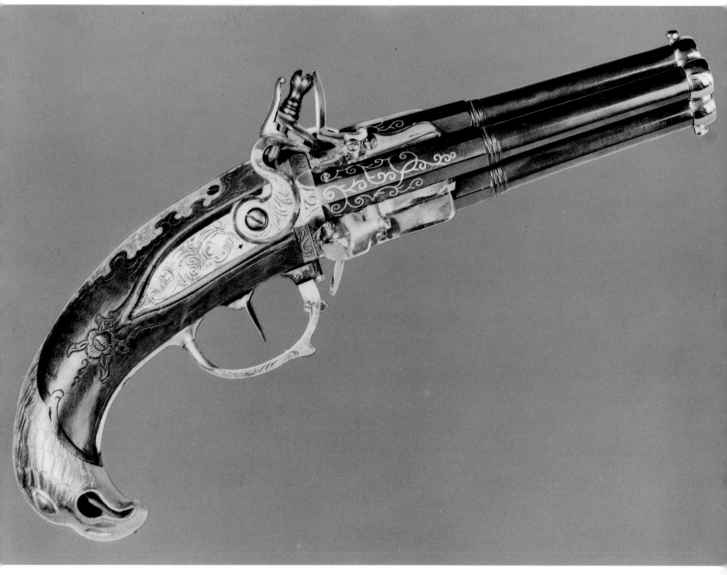

106 The combination of deeply blued barrels set against a brass-overlaid *tête d'oiseau* butt is particularly pleasing in this three-barrelled pistol made in Augsburg *c.* 1775

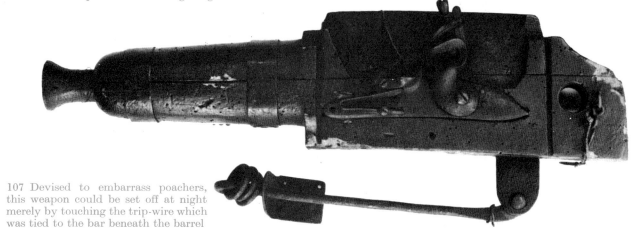

107 Devised to embarrass poachers, this weapon could be set off at night merely by touching the trip-wire which was tied to the bar beneath the barrel

108 English Light Dragoons demonstrate the method of loading, holding and firing carbines

DURING THE NINETEENTH century in England a revolution in the firearms industry occurred which facilitated the transformation of the flintlock into the automatic cartridge-loaded firearm still used universally today. This achievement had been made possible by the enthusiastic research of English, European and American gunsmiths into the development of the percussion form of ignition and a cartridge that would incorporate both charge and detonator.

The inventions of a Scottish clergyman, the Reverend John Forsyth, had a contagious effect on his contemporaries. Minister of the parish of Belhevie in Aberdeenshire, Forsyth had learnt the elements of mechanics at University, and in his home-made laboratory had experimented with a substance known as fulminates of mercury, which when struck would detonate. (For some time past this chemical had been experimented with in relation to firearms, but was considered to be too potent. Berthollet, a pre-revolutionary French scientist, had tried mixing a similar chemical, potassium chlorate, with other ingredients in an attempt to strengthen the consistency of gunpowder, but had given up for a similar reason — that processing in any large quantities proved too dangerous).

Throughout 1805 Forsyth was testing a form of ignition by percussion; this proved so successful that the following year he travelled to London to try to interest the sporting world in his invention. Eventually Lord Moira, Master-General of the Ordnance, asked Forsyth to take over a workshop in the Tower of London for further experiments.

Though at first he applied his invention only to sporting guns [figure 110], Forsyth must have foreseen its application to military arms, and that his percussion lock would prove a more satisfactory form of ignition than the flintlock which, even in its most developed form, could be uncertain in adverse weather conditions. For a year Forsyth was left undisturbed to work on the solution to the problem of mixing a compound that would not damage the fulminates container on the lock. After several minor accidents he was successful. Unfortunately Moira was replaced by Lord Chatham who, without any consideration, cancelled Forsyth's allowance and prevented him from using the Tower for his work. England was at this time at war with France. News of Forsyth's invention reached Napoleon who offered him a large sum for his lock mechanism. Fortunately for Chatham's reputation and for England's fortunes in the war against France, Forsyth refused. No longer patronised by the government, Forsyth was determined to patent his invention, and having opened a shop in London, profited from the sales of his gun.

His guns are easily recognised by the odd shape of the lock. The fulminates container resembles a scent bottle, the lower half of which was filled with detonating powder. This pivoted on a screw, and when revolved allowed a small quantity of priming charge to leak through a small

109 (below) Manton's tube lock had only a restricted circulation, though it was more reliable than Forsyth's 'Scent Bottle' lock

110 (above) A sporting version of Forsyth's 'Scent Bottle' made popular by wildfowlers during the Regency

hole cut in the partition which separated the magazine from the flash pan positioned in the top half. The force of the cock hitting the spring firing pin detonated the powder which in turn ignited the main charge.

Forsyth and Company flourished until 1821 when their patent expired, but although his was a highly advanced form of ignition there was a constant danger that the loose powder in the lower half of the 'scent bottle' would be ignited by a flash from the pan. Other English gunsmiths — although having solutions to this problem —were unable to market their own adaptations of Forsyth's lock until 1821. By placing the powder in a pellet the danger of igniting a magazine was overcome [figure 115].

Samuel Pauly, an engineer of Swiss extraction working in Paris, patented a centre-fire breech-loading cartridge

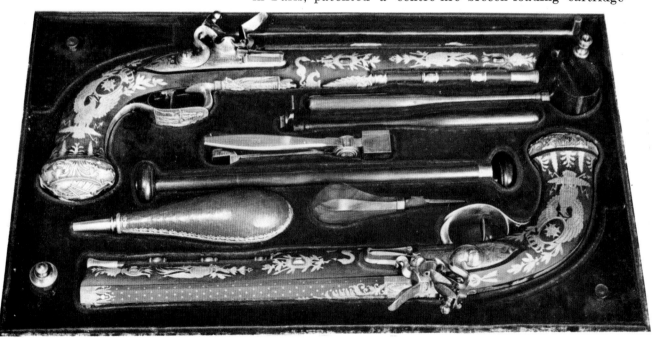

111 A specially commissioned pair of pistols by Boutet complete with accessories in their case

112 (*opposite*) A Turkish chamois leather double holster decorated with silver thread and an Indo-Persian concentric powder-horn with gold mounts

firearm in 1812 in which the cartridge was re-loaded [figure 117]. This system was brought to Napoleon's notice but he did not altogether approve of it. Although Pauly's guns could be fired with great rapidity compared with the flintlock musket then in general use, they were expensive to produce. If this invention had been submitted in 1807, when the secret of Forsyth's lock was in such demand in France, and the sequence of victories had provided the treasury with extra funds, it would probably have been adopted. Immediately after the fall of Paris in 1814, Pauly left France for London — the undisputed centre of the firearms industry.

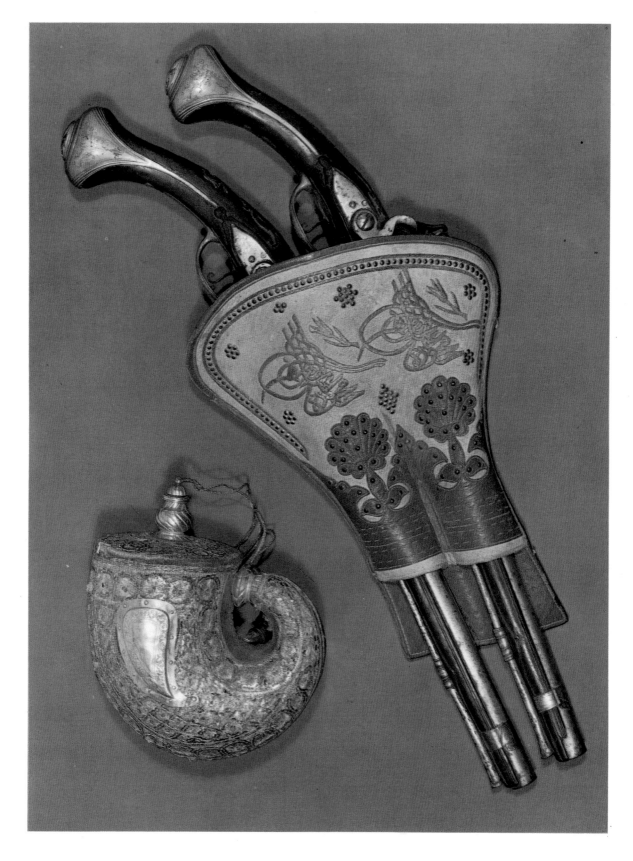

113 A fowling-piece by Pauly with the enclosed action open for loading, and the butt-trap open also

114 Military pistols were sometimes fitted with shoulder-stocks in order to ensure greater accuracy; this example has been converted from flintlock to percussion

Typically French in form, Pauly's pistols had drop barrels. Loading was a simple operation. First the brass cartridge was inserted in the breech, and after the barrel had been elevated into alignment with the lock, the enclosed action was cocked by means of an exterior cocking lever. While testing this and other pieces by Pauly the Société d'Encouragement pour l'Industrie Nationale reported that among the weapon's many advantages, it was impossible to load it twice — a mistake frequently made with muzzle loading guns [figure 113] — and that its enclosed action was a protection against rain and damp.

On arriving in England Pauly settled down quickly and started experimenting with compressed air ignition. Airguns had been in use in the eighteenth century, but Pauly harnessed the power of compressed air so that instead of merely ejecting the bullet it generated enough heat to ignite an explosive contained in the rear end of a cartridge. Before, however, very many of these guns had been manufactured, Pauly turned his attention to a project in no way connected with guns. Incorrigibly inventive, he joined forces with a compatriot, the famous gunmaker to George III, Durs Egg, in a balloon-making venture. Partly owing to the end of the war (which had been a perpetual source of income for gunmakers), lack of funds compelled them to give up their plans to put 'Dolphin', a fish-shaped balloon, in the air.

Although Pauly's guns did not encroach upon Forsyth's patent, they never became popular in England. Meanwhile

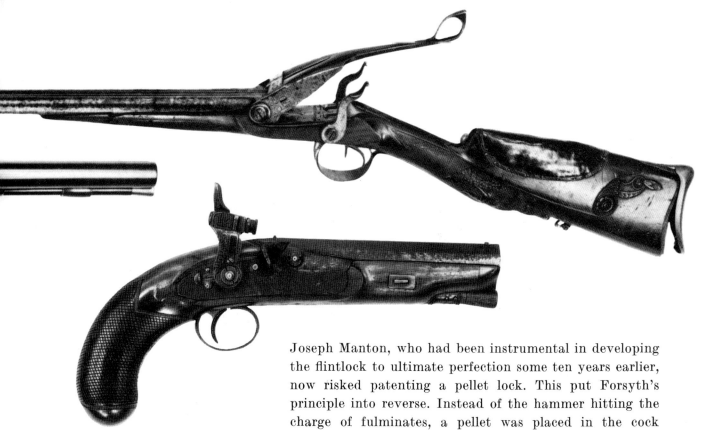

115 An inversion of Forsyth's percussion principle, Manton's Pellet lock was an unsuccessful attempt to render Forsyth's patent superfluous

Joseph Manton, who had been instrumental in developing the flintlock to ultimate perfection some ten years earlier, now risked patenting a pellet lock. This put Forsyth's principle into reverse. Instead of the hammer hitting the charge of fulminates, a pellet was placed in the cock which fell down on the nipple, thus causing an ignition. But as loading procedure took even longer than the 'scent bottle' there was no great demand for these guns. Manton next experimented with a copper tube filled with fulminates of mercury which was placed in the pan and held by a hinged cover [figure 109], specially cut so as to let the sharpened hammer cut the tube when it fell. Although entirely successful, Manton was forced to give it up after losing a lawsuit brought against him by Forsyth. Shortly after this Forsyth left London for Scotland, never to return, leaving the scene set and ready for the Patent Race which started the moment after his own had expired.

The chief disadvantage of locks at this time was the multitude of component parts that slowed the loading process. The true percussion cap, which only needed to be placed on a tube or nipple to act as a support for the falling hammer, was invented by a painter called Joshua Shaw, who because he could not patent his invention in England, took it to America around 1816, where it was very readily accepted. In its earliest form the cap was made out of steel, like Pauly's cartridges, being re-primed after every shot; soon however copper replaced steel and the cap was disposed of after it had been used once.

By 1825 percussion arms were used by the majority of sportsmen in England, but some still preferred the flintlock, which continued to be made. Those who could not afford new guns from the Bond Street and Piccadilly gunmakers had their flintlock fowling pieces converted into percussion caps by removing the frizzen pan and steel, and replacing them with a nipple set in a plug [figure 114]. Occasionally one comes across good quality guns mod-

116 An English reply to Colt's invasion of the London market: Adams' revolver, gold plated and contained in a velvet-lined presentation case

82

ernised in this manner, probably because their owners had got used to shooting with them and did not want to give them up. (On the other hand, collectors should be careful to examine what appears to be a flintlock in order to determine whether it has been converted to percussion cap and back again by some insensitive person, in order to increase its value as an antique. A close look at the frizzen pan to see if it has been re-welded, at the lockplate

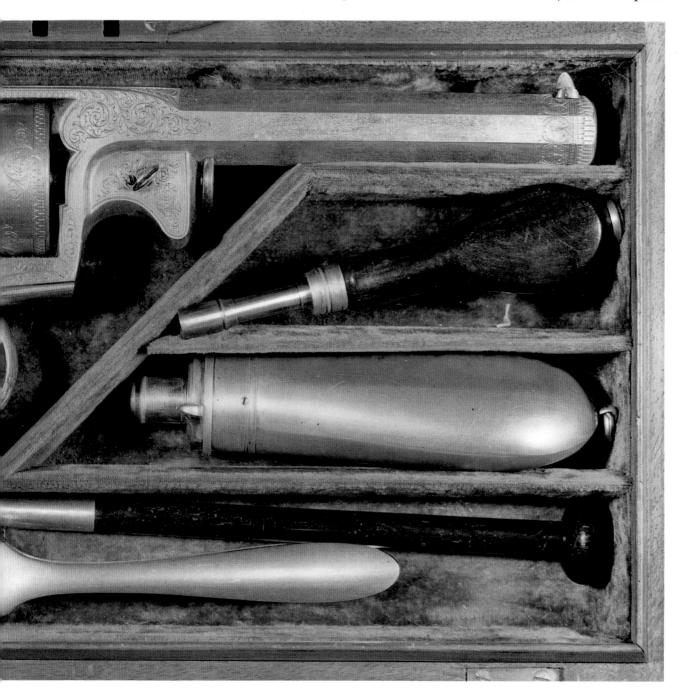

117 Pauly's pistol with drop barrel, perhaps half a century in advance of its time

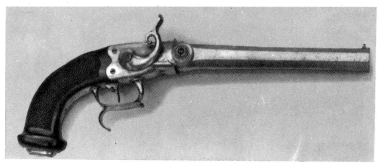

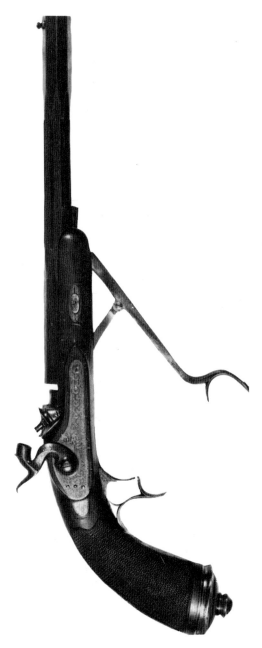

118 Renette continued to make target pistols until the 1870's; this model is breech-loading with a sliding barrel

and at the barrel to find out whether the plug has been removed and the hole filled, will settle any doubts. Fortunately such freaks are rare owing to the expense involved in this operation).

Although the percussion cap was popular among private gun owners by 1825, it had to wait a long time before a decision was taken to apply it to regulation pattern fire-arms. In 1805 the Baker flintlock rifle had been issued to selected troops, but it had not proved entirely satisfactory. Accuracy was the most important consideration, and it was too easily assumed that this short-barrelled rifle would be a tremendous improvement on the Brown Bess. The Kentucky rifle was a success because the patched bullet lay firmly in the grooves and by the time it reached the muzzle of the rather long barrel it had achieved maximum velocity. But European armies still clung to large-bored guns, and Baker himself was ready to admit that if the twist in rifling was increased so as to make the bullet spin faster and fly more accurately it would require an even longer bore to give increased velocity and thus prevent the bullet from riding over or stripping the grooves. The result was a clumsy weapon which because of the difficulty in loading was only about as practical as a musket.

Gunsmiths in England and America, who were busy developing new types of ignition infinitely better than those in use in the armed service, both experienced considerable frustration as a result of their differences with official bodies such as the Board of Ordnance in England set up to examine new weapons. After the Napoleonic wars the Tower of London was stocked with regulation pattern muskets which the Board of Ordnance was very reluctant to scrap. When, however, the Board came under the direction of Mr Lovell, tests were carried out to compare the flintlock with the percussion cap. The first of these tests, in 1834, was probably forced on the Government

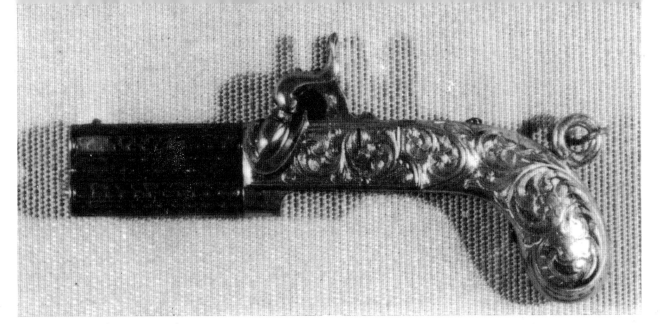

119 A miniature percussion cap pistol about two inches long

by Forsyth who wanted to impress on them the obvious differences between the two locks. The 1834 tests were carried out in all types of weather, and no less than six thousand rounds were fired. There could be no grounds for doubting the superiority of the new form of ignition, for the result showed that the flintlock had misfired nine hundred and twenty-two times against only thirty-six misfires from the percussion cap. But although these tests must have impressed the Board of Ordnance, the army was not re-equipped with percussion cap rifles until two years later.

This new rifle, designed by an officer in the Brunswick Army after which it was named, proved to be one of the worst weapons ever issued to the armed forces. The soldiers discovered, much to their discomfort, that there was additional recoil with this large-bore rifle and that not only was it difficult to aim straight, but the charge did not provide enough power to keep the bullet spinning in flight. In 1841 the armoury in the Tower of London was partially destroyed by fire and several thousand flintlock guns perished. This conflagration helped to dispose of old stock so that when detachments were equipped they were armed with newly designed rifles.

Gradually the designers realised that a solution to the problem posed by rifling could be found in the bullet. Various types had been tried out with a view to eliminating air resistance. A 'belted' spherical bullet was developed for use with a Brunswick rifle but this only half solved the problem. The famous gunsmith William Greener in

1836 tried to make a self-expanding bullet which would fit tightly into the grooves but would not require too powerful a push with a ram-rod. He designed a conical bullet with a flat end into which was inserted a wedge-shaped wooden plug. When the bullet was fired the explosion forced this plug further into the bullet, thus causing the head to expand. But Greener was not able to persuade the Government to adopt his bullet; instead he received a monetary reward some twenty years later after the Minie bullet had been accepted. Colonel Minie's bullet was similar·to Greener's. Instead of using a wooden plug, Minie, an instructor at Vincennes, adopted one made of iron. The four-groove rifle designed to fire this bullet was at once used by the French army, but the British Government was quick to step in and buy the rights. The Minie rifle, though replacing the Brunswick and used with effect during the Kaffir War of 1846-52, was in turn superseded by the Enfield which had proved its superiority in trials conducted in the early fifties [figure 121].

Hardly any reference has been made to revolvers, which were produced from time to time in the seventeenth and eighteenth centuries, but owing to their dangers never in any great quantity, with the result that they are comparatively rare today. Quite often a burst chamber caused by a gas leak induced many of their original owners to discard them. During the seventeenth century when, out of curiosity, repeating systems were being experimented with in England, a few gunsmiths turned their efforts to producing a pistol with a revolving chamber. A snaphaunce petronel, a large pistol of ingenious construction made in England about 1650, survives in one piece because of its stout construction [figure 122]. But the manufacture of the revolver remained comparatively unknown, and only a handful of gunsmiths had any success until the early nineteenth century when Elisha Collier, an American, tackled the problem in a new and productive way [figure 124].

Collier overcame the difficult problem of leaking gasses by fitting the chamber on to an extension of the barrel. In order to be rotated the cylinder had to be drawn back manually and turned until the next chamber was in alignment, when the force of the spring compelled this chamber to fit tightly over the end of the barrel. This

120 Currier shows two American wild fowlers on the bank of the Delaware River using double-barrelled percussion cap fowling-pieces

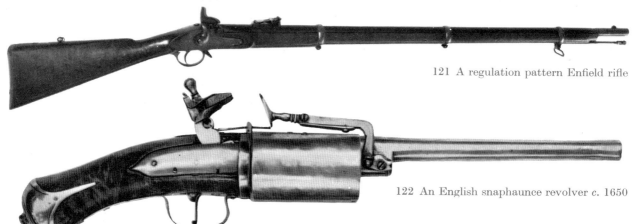

121 A regulation pattern Enfield rifle

122 An English snaphaunce revolver c. 1650

123 Colonel Samuel Colt, the first mass producer of firearms

ensured that the gas should not leak into the remaining chambers. Using a magazine priming mechanism, set in a container behind the steel, Collier eliminated the necessity of having a separate pan for each chamber. A ratchet and pawl system automatically distributed the priming charge when the cover was closed. These two remarkable innovations made this revolver quite safe to handle, but because it was expensive Collier found that he had a better chance of marketing it in England than in America, and in 1811 he crossed the Atlantic and set up a business in the Strand in London.

With the introduction of the percussion cap the mechanism of the revolver could be simplified and condensed. Of the many gunsmiths working on the revolver during the eighteen-thirties, the first that comes to mind is Samuel Colt. Born in 1814 in Hartford, Connecticut, Colt left home when he was young, and refusing his father's offer of an apprenticeship in the silk trade, joined the crew of the brig *Corvo* and sailed to India. Since most of Collier's flintlock revolvers had been exported to India by the Government it is probable that Colt saw examples of these in Calcutta. Though we cannot be sure of this, we do know that on his way back to America Colt applied the principle of the ratchet, probably inspired by a paddle-steamer wheel, to the cylinder of a percussion cap revolver he had carved in wood. Colt arranged for experimental models to be made by a gunsmith called Anton Chase and his assistant John Pearson, and in order to pay for these experiments he organised a series of lectures in different States in which he demonstrated the effect of laughing gas. Charging up to thirty cents for an entrance fee, he was able to send Pearson considerable sums of money, at the same time giving instruction in the manufacture of revolvers and shotguns. Satisfied with the results of

124 (*above*) A Collier flintlock revolver

125 (*right*) An English percussion cap 'pepper box' revolver, popular from *c*. 1835 until *c*. 1850

Pearson's work, Colt travelled to England and France to patent his revolver.

On his return to America, Colt started a new series of lectures; at one given at the Baltimore Museum he met the Director, Joseph Walker, and told him about his inventions. This resulted in a modest commission from a cousin of Walker, who was an army captain. Colt was not making much money at this time and his partnership with Pearson broke up for this reason. Production was therefore transferred to the Patent Arms Manufacturing Company of New Jersey which made revolvers in three different styles [figure 128]. This happy state continued only until 1845 when the Company went bankrupt. Luckily for Colt, a year later the United States went to war with Mexico, and gunsmiths were again in business. Colt revolvers had been used by Captain Walker some ten years before, who, recognising their importance, persuaded the Government to order a thousand revolvers for the Dragoons. Eli Witney manufactured these heavy military pistols which proved so successful that another thousand were ordered. But by this time Colt, who had his own plant at Hartford, was able to undertake the order without the necessity of using Witney as a sub-contractor. The Dragoon pistol, though an admirable weapon for mounted soldiers was unsuitable for infantry because of its weight [figure 128]. In 1857 the first Navy Revolver appeared. Having the same barrel length as the Dragoon it was considerably lighter and of thirty-six calibre. It owed its name to an engraving on the

126 The Colt revolving rifle *c.* 1836, from the plant at Paterson, New Jersey

127 Robert Adams loading Prince Albert's revolver with a lever ramrod

cylinder of warships fighting at sea. It is interesting to compare this with the pocket model revolver produced a year later [figure 129], which had a similar engraving of a coach hold-up scene engraved by William Ormsby.

Colt always kept to single-action mechanism on his muzzle-loaded firearms; there were comparatively few component parts. No lock springs, however, could indefinitely endure the rough treatment and continual use which they were put to in the armed forces, and spares produced at Hartford were distributed to Colt's agencies in America, as well as to the troops.

Colt came to England for the Great Exhibition of 1851 hoping that the English, who had not taken readily to the earlier forms of revolver, might be interested in his own model. He thought that by merely bringing with him several cased presentation revolvers with ivory butts and extravagant engraving he would dazzle the English firearms industry. Much to his surprise Robert Adams [figure 127], an Englishman, had already exhibited a double-action revolver comparable to his own. The coincidence of Colt's arrival with that of the new English pistol gave emphasis to their rivalry. What distinguished the two different types of pistol was their action. Samuel Colt, who was now a colonel, always favoured single action, whilst Robert Adams' revolvers were fitted with a double action. A single-action revolver has to be thumb-cocked, but by 'fanning' or palming the hammer with the trigger held back it could be fired very rapidly. This way of shooting

128 The Colt Dragoon pistol which proved its superiority in the Mexican War

129 (*right*) An 1849 Colt Pocket Revolver in wooden case together with bullet mould, powder flask and cap box

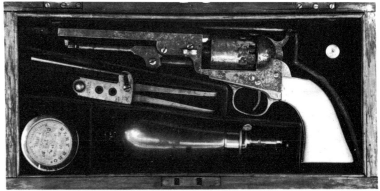

130 An infantryman from a series of engravings of the English militia by Scott,
executed in 1797

a revolver was popular in the wilds of America, where a
practised man could fire all six shots in less than four
seconds. With the Adams revolver one could either cock
the action by pulling the trigger or else cock it by thumb.

131 Made at Tula after the Crimean War, this Russian piece is a tribute to the Adams revolver

132 Loading instructions together with an advertisement which Colt printed for inclusion in all his London-made cased revolvers

In a surprise attack the latter movement was found to be particularly useful, it being easier to pull a trigger without first having to draw back the hammer with one's thumb. Even 'fanning' delayed ejection.

Adams, in conjunction with the Deane brothers, produced revolvers in five sizes until 1855 when they were greatly improved by Captain Beaumont's invention, which enabled the Adams revolver to be either single or double action. During this time, however, Colt had set up in England soon after the Great Exhibition, and established a factory in Pimlico, which produced Navy and pocket model revolvers [figure 132]. These can be distinguished from American models by the London address stamped on top of the barrel and the proof marks which appear not only on the barrel but on each chamber. The English seemed to prefer the Adams revolver in spite of the fact that the Government had placed an order with Colt for pistols to be supplied to the Navy, and when Beaumont's invention helped to perfect the Adams revolver still further, Colt, finding his Pimlico works superfluous, shipped mechanics and machinery back to America. Only his Agency remained in Pall Mall. It was during the arduous campaigns in the Crimea that Colt's pistols were discovered to be more reliable than Adams'. A double-action revolver required many more component parts than a single-action pistol. The ratchet system was quite complicated — the pieces having to be thinly made in order to be accommodated in such a confined space, with the result that they tended to break more easily, and were difficult to repair. But there were enough of both types of pistol to satisfy any taste in firearms. After 1856 the demand for Colt revolvers slackened, and feeling the threat of new patents Colt decided to withdraw from his expensive venture. He was, moreover, dismayed to find that compared with the Americas England was a law-abiding land: strikes were unheard of, civilians did not arm, and guns (except for military purposes) were in small demand. But the English were not unaffected by his visit; he taught them mass production, and from 1856 onwards the demand for the work of the individual gunsmith diminished.

Commissions for service pattern weapons were given to the factories at Enfield, and except for the companies which continued to produce revolvers the smaller ones had to content themselves with sporting guns and rifles.

The Enfield rifle, which had been issued to the troops before all detachments had received the Minie rifle, incorporated all the best features of a series of new rifle designs submitted to the Board of Ordnance by a group of leading gunsmiths. Superior to any earlier rifle, the Enfield is better known as the chief cause of the Indian Mutiny. It fired a cartridge lubricated with grease made, so it was rumoured, from cow and pig fat, which, since the Hindu troops regarded the cow as sacred and the pig as the most degraded of all animals, involved an outrage upon Hindu susceptibilities and taboos.

In 1861, at the beginning of the American Civil War, the Confederate States had to import firearms from Europe, since they possessed only a few gun factories. No less than seventy thousand Enfields were sent across the Atlantic. England's sympathies lay more with the Southern States after two Southern ministers, travelling to London in order to trade cotton and gold for arms, were arrested on the English ship *Trent* by a Yankee Man-o'-War in mid-Atlantic. But a French-born New Orleans doctor, Jean LeMat, contrived to reach France where he arranged for five thousand revolvers of his own design to be made by M. Girard et Fils. Although this nine-shot revolver with a central bore for buck shot infringed Colt's European patents, no action was taken, and they were delivered to the Confederacy having first been proved in London. But by far the most popular arm was the Colt Navy revolver, copies of which were made with considerable difficulty in a cotton mill by Giles Griswold and his brother-in-law, Colonel Grier.

Samuel Colt died in 1862. He did not live to see the Frontier revolver or the Winchester lever-action repeating rifle of 1873, which was so widely used by the settlers that it became known as the gun which won the west. In England and America from 1850-60, the last years of the percussion cap, breech-loading rifles and carbines appeared from time to time in the armies. In 1855 the Terry Carbine made by a company in Birmingham was put on the market: the breech was opened by a bolt-action which was fitted to rifles. It was a 'capping carbine', *i.e.* the cartridge contained only the bullet and charge,

133 A Colt 'Stand of flags' stamped copper powder flask

134 (*left*) Jacob Snider's conversion applied to an Enfield rifle 135 (*right*) An English Westley-Richards 'monkey-tail' carbine

the detonator or cap being placed on the nipple. This was used in great quantities by the Confederate Army, but its breech mechanism was not as strong as that of its American counterpart. In 1848 Christian Sharps invented a carbine with a falling breech-block mechanism, lowered by an under-barrel lever, which also formed the trigger guard; the forerunner of the Henry Martini action which is still in use today, it was simple to operate. Loading was accelerated by the addition of the tape primer, invented by and named after a dentist called Maynard. Rather similar to a roll of caps used in a modern toy pistol, the priming tape was kept in a small compartment which was open near the top of the nipple. In the late 1850's the 'Emigrant Aid Company' was formed in Massachusetts and New England to introduce settlers into Kansas who were opposed to slavery. Consequently many armed fights took place between the supporters of of slavery and the new settlers. Lawrence, the town in which the latter had established themselves, was rather badly damaged, and, in revenge, John Brown (about whom the Unionist song was written), supported by his sons and some Emigrant Aid Company settlers armed with Sharps' carbines, attacked and killed the most ardent supporters of the slave state. (It was at this time that twenty-five Sharps' carbines were given to the settlers by a minister of the Plymouth, Congregationalist Church in Brooklyn, New York, Henry Ward Beecher, after which they were known as 'Beecher's Bibles'). John Brown was hanged after he attempted to take over the Arsenal at Harpers Ferry, and the only reminder we have today of Sharps' carbine is the phrase 'sharps-shooter'.

In England the Princes patent carbine, with an under-barrel lever which drew the barrel forward to expose the breech, and the Terry carbine were displaced by the more successful Westley Richards 'monkey-tail' carbine, which had a simplified action. It fired Terry carbine cartridges and was officially adopted by the cavalry in 1861. Although the Snider was adopted by the Government soon afterwards, the Westley Richards monkey-tail carbine was used as late as the Boer War by some Australian units in the Imperial Army [figure 135]. Breechloading improvements had been encouraged by the Government since 1850, in view of the fact that two years before the Germans had equipped their troops with a needle gun which had a bolt action. This was really the first modern gun, and it proved

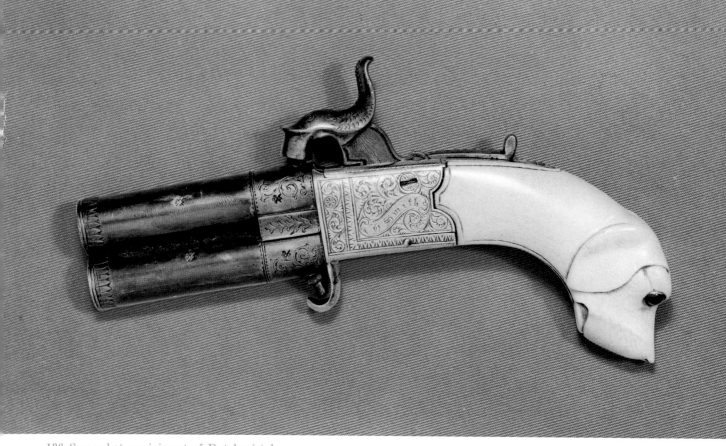

136 Somewhat reminiscent of Dutch pistols produced in the seventeenth century, this mid-nineteenth-century English percussion cap pocket pistol has a beagle's head ivory butt

137 (below) A Romantic portrait of Samuel Whawell

its efficiency in 1866 in the Austro-Prussian War. In spite of this emphasis on breech-loaders, only the cavalry was equipped with the Westley Richards carbine, the rest of the troops carried Enfields. The only obvious way in which the entire army could be equipped with breech-loading guns without great expense was by the conversion of existing stock; and so a Committee in 1864 examined designs submitted by different gunsmiths. The most successful was found to be Jacob Snider's system, where the breech-block was hinged to the side and could be opened by pressing a sprung thumb-piece. The firing pin passed from the nipple to the front where it projected a fraction through the face of the breech.

Since Pauly had made considerable advances in experimenting with metallic cartridges, little had been achieved in this field until the paper cartridge with a brass base was found to be unsuitable for the Snider. On the Continent the needle fire system invented by Dreyse, a Prussian gunsmith who had at one time been a student under Pauly, had been in use since 1848, but because of the disturbing way in which breech and barrel became easily fouled and

95

138 A forgery of a sixteenth-century wheel lock pistol, made for a nineteenth-century collector; certain parts are missing and the craftsmanship is inferior

the needle corroded it was not adopted in England. Eventually Colonel Boxer, an Englishman, designed a brass-enclosed cartridge which solved these problems.

Muzzle-loading guns were now replaced by breech-loading guns, except in remote areas where they were in use until recent times. Towards the end of the nineteenth century, military designers concentrated on producing an automatic gun which would obviate loading after each shot, since during this interval the shooter was most exposed to attack. First in the line of automatic weapons was the Borchardt pistol invented in 1893. Towards the end of the nineteenth century decorated pieces became rare and expensive. Today when gunsmiths are commissioned to make decorated pieces, nineteenth-century fowling motifs are used.

The collecting of firearms began with the craze for everything mediaeval, which started in the 1840's (when at a Court Ball at Buckingham Palace the French Ambassador wore, or so he claimed, the armour of Joan of Arc), and which induced the rich to collect indiscriminately arms and armour for the interior decoration of their houses. But the only firearms thought worthy of display at this period were those made before and during the golden age of armour in the sixteenth century. This craze indirectly brought about the formation of some of the most important national collections of arms in America, England

139 A superimposed charge could be fired without reloading in this Moutier Le-page Belgian rifle

140 This English percussion cap pistol was made more deadly by a spring bayonet which is released by a catch set on the side of the box lock

and France. It was during this time that Sir Richard Wallace managed to purchase most of the best pieces out of the Nieuwekerke, Spitzer and Meyrick Collections in the face of strong Continental opposition. He illustrated his trophies of arms in Hertford House where they now form the present Wallace Collection of Arms. Another Englishman, Samuel Whawell, who as a young man had learnt about armour when he had been compelled to supervise the family business of restoring 'ancient' armour, was employed by the millionaire Mr Edwin Brett to scour Europe in search of rare pieces. The Gayeski Collection, which he acquired from Poland, was removed in sleighs pursued by packs of starving wolves which could only be kept at bay by continuous firing. In 1893 he arranged the display of arms trophies in Hampton Court Palace and two years later consented to sit for his own portrait in a suit of sixteenth-century armour [figure 137]. Although the fashion for mediaeval decor declined in England during the twenties, it was popular in America until the death of that insatiable collector Mr William Randolph Hearst.

It is therefore through the patience and connoisseurship of these men that students of firearms are able to study some of the finest examples of Continental firearms in the Wallace Collection as well as the national collection at the Tower of London and the Royal Collection at Windsor Castle. In America the magnificent collection of early arms in the Metropolitan Museum is supported by the Winchester and Colt Collections in which later arms predominate.

It is significant, however, that all these and most of the other great private collections also were assembled after firearms had ceased to be the products of artists and decorative craftsmen.

On the Continent there are fine and important collections at the *Real Armeria* in Madrid; the Musée de l'Armée in Paris, where Napoleonic weapons are best represented; in the Armouries at Dresden, where there are particularly splendid sixteenth-century Saxon arms; and in the National Bavarian Museum in Munich.